BUDGET OF THE U.S. GOVERNMENT

A New Foundation for American Greatness

Fiscal Year 2018

D1621667

$37.00

EXECUTIVE OFFICE OF THE PRESIDENT OF THE UNITED STATES

OFFICE OF MANAGEMENT AND BUDGET

Budget of the United States Government, Fiscal Year 2018 contains the Budget Message of the President, information on the President's priorities, and summary tables.

Analytical Perspectives, Budget of the United States Government, Fiscal Year 2018 contains analyses that are designed to highlight specified subject areas or provide other significant presentations of budget data that place the budget in perspective. This volume includes economic and accounting analyses; information on Federal receipts and collections; analyses of Federal spending; information on Federal borrowing and debt; baseline or current services estimates; and other technical presentations.

GENERAL NOTES

1. All years referenced for budget data are fiscal years unless otherwise noted. All years referenced for economic data are calendar years unless otherwise noted.

2. At the time of this writing, only one of the annual appropriations bills for 2017 had been enacted (the Military Construction and Veterans Affairs Appropriations Act), as well as the Further Continuing and Security Assistance Appropriations Act, which provided 2017 discretionary funding for certain Department of Defense accounts; therefore, the programs provided for in the remaining 2017 annual appropriations bills were operating under a continuing resolution (Public Law 114-223, division C, as amended). For these programs, references to 2017 spending in the text and tables reflect the levels provided by the continuing resolution.

3. Detail in this document may not add to the totals due to rounding.

ISBN: 978-159888-953-6

Table of Contents

THE BUDGET MESSAGE OF THE PRESIDENT

To the Congress of the United States:

On February 28, I spoke to a joint session of the Congress about what we need to do to begin a new chapter of American Greatness. I asked the Nation to look forward nine years and imagine the wonders we could achieve by America's 250th anniversary of our Independence if we set free the dreams of our people by removing the barriers holding back our economic growth.

This Budget's defining ambition is to unleash the dreams of the American people. This requires laying a new foundation for American Greatness.

Through streamlined Government, we will drive an economic boom that raises incomes and expands job opportunities for all Americans. Faster economic growth, coupled with fiscal restraint, will enable us to fully fund our national priorities, balance our budget, and start to pay down our national debt.

Our moral commitment to replacing our current economic stagnation with faster economic growth rests on the following eight pillars of reform:

Health Reform. We need to enable Americans to buy the healthcare they need at a price they can afford. To this end, we must repeal Obamacare and its burdensome regulations and mandates, and replace it with a framework that restores choice and competition. This will lower the cost of care so that more Americans can get the medical attention they need. Additionally, Medicaid, which inadequately serves enrollees and taxpayers, must be reformed to allow States to manage their own programs, with continued financial support from the Federal Government.

Tax Reform and Simplification. We must reduce the tax burden on American workers and businesses, so that we can maximize incomes and economic growth. We must also simplify our tax system, so that individuals and businesses do not waste countless hours and resources simply paying their taxes.

Immigration Reform. We must reform immigration policy so that it serves our national interest. We will adopt commonsense proposals that protect American workers, reduce burdens on taxpayers and public resources, and focus Federal funds on underserved and disadvantaged citizens.

Reductions in Federal Spending. We must scrutinize every dollar the Federal Government spends. Just as families decide how to manage limited budgets, we must ensure the Federal Government spends precious taxpayer dollars only on our highest national priorities, and always in the most efficient, effective manner.

Regulatory Rollback. We must eliminate every outdated, unnecessary, or ineffective Federal regulation, and move aggressively to build regulatory frameworks that stimulate—rather than stagnate—job creation. Even for those regulations we must leave in place, we must strike every provision that is counterproductive, ineffective, or outdated.

American Energy Development. We must increase development of America's energy resources, strengthening our national security, lowering the price of electricity and transportation fuels, and driving down the cost of consumer goods so that every American individual and business has more money to save and invest. A consistent, long-term supply of lower-cost American energy brings with it a much larger economy, more jobs, and greater security for the American people.

Welfare Reform. We must reform our welfare system so that it does not discourage able-bodied adults from working, which takes away scarce resources from those in real need. Work must be the center of our social policy.

Education Reform. We need to return decisions regarding education back to the State and local levels, while advancing opportunities for parents and students to choose, from all available options, the school that best fits their needs to learn and succeed.

***

To unleash the power of American work and creativity—and drive opportunity and faster economic growth—we must reprioritize Federal spending so that it advances the safety and security of the American people.

This Budget, therefore, includes $639 billion for the Department of Defense—a $52 billion increase from the 2017 annualized continuing resolution level. This increase will be offset by targeted reductions elsewhere. This defense funding is vital to rebuilding, modernizing, and preparing our Armed Forces for the future so that our military remains the world's preeminent fighting force and we can continue to ensure peace through strength. This Budget also increases funding to take care of our great veterans, who have served their country with such honor and distinction.

The Budget also meets the need to materially increase funding for border security, immigration enforcement, and law enforcement at the Departments of Homeland Security and Justice. These funding increases will provide additional resources for a southern border wall, expanded detention capacity, and initiatives to reduce violent crime, as well as more immigration judges, U.S. Immigration and Customs Enforcement officers, and Border Patrol agents. The Budget also invests significant resources in efforts to combat opioid abuse.

In these dangerous times, our increased attention to public safety and national security sends a clear message to the world—a message of American strength and resolve. It follows through on my promise to focus on keeping Americans safe, keeping terrorists out of our Nation, and putting violent offenders behind bars.

As this Budget returns us to economic prosperity, it will also allow us to fund additional priorities, including infrastructure, student loan reform, and initiatives to help working families such as paid parental leave. We will champion the hardworking taxpayers who have been ignored for too long. Once we end our economic stagnation and return to robust growth, so many of our aspirations will be within reach.

It is now up to the Congress to act. I pledge my full cooperation in ending the economic malaise that has, for too long, crippled the dreams of our people. The time for small thinking is over. As we look forward to our 250th year, I am calling upon all Members of Congress to join me in striving to do big and bold and daring things for our Nation. We have it in our power to set free the dreams of our people. Let us begin.

DONALD J. TRUMP

THE WHITE HOUSE,
MAY 23, 2017

A NEW FOUNDATION FOR AMERICAN GREATNESS

I. OVERVIEW

This 2018 Budget lays the groundwork for an overdue renewal of the American spirit, and provides a detailed and specific roadmap to get us there. *A New Foundation for American Greatness* is not just the title of this Budget. It is a bold and specific set of policy and budgetary initiatives that tackle many of the problems ignored or exacerbated by previous administrations.

Our Nation must make substantial changes to the policies and spending priorities of the previous administration if our citizens are to be safe and prosperous in the future. This Budget represents an attainable vision of a Government that preserves the safety and fiscal security of this Nation while enabling the creativity and drive that has always supported the American Dream. This New Foundation for American Greatness presents an opportunity for our Nation's values and constitutional principles to send a message of American strength, leadership, and fiscal responsibility to the rest of the world.

This message comes from a place of profound respect for the American people and the hardworking taxpayers who built this Nation. It reflects President Donald J. Trump's deep commitment to restore this Nation's greatness, a rejection of the failed status quo, and an effort that strives to be worthy of the American people and the trust they have placed in the President.

With a $20 trillion debt threatening generations of American prosperity, our Federal budget must spend every dollar effectively, efficiently, and in ways that make a demonstrable difference for our Nation. It also must do something equally important: lay the foundation for a rebuilt national defense, strengthened borders, and the long-term soundness of our economy and well-being of the American family.

The President and this Budget aim to achieve this by laying:

- A new foundation that solidifies our commitment to the border's security.

- A new foundation of policies to produce new American jobs.

- A new foundation for immigration policy that serves the national interest and the American taxpayer.

- A new foundation of federalism that trusts States to help manage America's health care.

- A new foundation that creates a pathway to welfare reform that is focused on promoting work and lifting people out of poverty.

- A new foundation that places America first by returning more American dollars home and ensuring foreign aid supports American interests and values.

- A new foundation that spurs innovation and enables the American worker and family to thrive.

- A new foundation of restraint that limits Government regulation and intrusion.

- A new foundation of discipline that puts our budget on a path to balance.

- And, a new foundation of focus on the forgotten American worker who now has an advocate in the Oval Office.

The time is now to address the fundamental challenges facing our Nation. It is more than just words on pages; it is a call to action to save this great Nation. We have borrowed from our children and their future for too long, the devastating consequences of which cannot be overstated. We are fast approaching having publicly held debt at or exceeding 100 percent of our Gross Domestic Product (GDP), a point at which hopes for a more prosperous future are irrevocably lost.

This Budget makes it clear that we will reverse the damaging trends from previous administrations and restore the American Dream. The New Foundation for American Greatness will put our Nation's budget back into balance and begin to reduce the national debt.

A New Foundation for American Greatness requires a new approach to how we tax, regulate, and support our American worker and job creators. A new approach to how we provide for the common defense and promote the general welfare. A new approach to how we care for the sick and educate our young. A new approach to how we spend every tax dollar.

The President believes it will take courage and bold leadership to restore our Nation's greatness. This Budget is a large and bold reversal from the spiral of decline we were on toward a more bright and prosperous future.

II. WHAT WENT WRONG: INHERITING $20 TRILLION IN DEBT AND A BROKEN, STAGNANT ECONOMY

The new Administration inherited an economic situation in which the United States is $20 trillion in debt and yet at the same time dramatically underserving the needs of its citizens due to a broken, stagnant economy.

The previous administration's economic policies resulted in a near doubling of the national debt from $10.6 trillion in 2009 to nearly $20 trillion in 2016. The amount of this debt that is publicly held—that is, the portion that requires financing on the capital markets—is $14 trillion. Relative to the economy, publicly held debt at the end of last fiscal year was 77 percent of GDP, nearly double the level of 39 percent of GDP eight years earlier. This run-up in debt over the last eight years brought it to a level that we have not seen since shortly after World War II.

While our national debt has soared, our economic growth has been historically abysmal.

Stagnant economic growth has severely weakened our Nation's capacity to pay off the debt in the future, especially as measured against historic norms. Overall growth of the economy was subpar even before the last recession and recovery from that recession has been weak.

From World War II to 2007, the average fourth quarter-over-fourth quarter growth rate was 3.5 percent. Over the last nine years, average growth has been 1.3 percent.

Productivity growth is also down from historical averages. Productivity growth (defined as growth in real output per labor hour) has averaged 0.5 percent per year over 2011-2016. Over the years 1948 to 2007, average annual productivity growth was 2.3 percent. This stagnation has left hardworking taxpayers and American families feeling like the American Dream is out of their reach.

SOURCES OF ECONOMIC STAGNATION

Trade Deals That Have Exported American Jobs. All across America, there are cities and towns devastated by unfair trade policies. Horrible trade deals from prior administrations have stripped wealth and jobs from our Nation. Persistent trade deficits go hand in hand with a stagnant recovery and our trade deficits have increased: net exports were about -1 percent of GDP in the early 1990s; they were -3.4 percent of GDP in 2016.

Burdensome Federal Regulation. Until the new Administration took office this year, the regulatory state had continued to grow and impede growth in the economy. For example, over the 10 years ending in 2016, non-independent agencies added between $78-$115 billion in estimated annual costs through the finalization of new regulations. This included several environmental regulations, such as the Light Duty Fuel Economy regulations and the Power Plant Mercury regulations that each had estimated compliance costs approaching or exceeding $10 billion per year. The true impact of regulations during this time was undoubtedly higher, as regulations issued by the so-called "independent agencies" are not included in this total. These "independent agencies" issue the majority of burdensome financial regulations, including the vast majority of the cost of compliance with the Dodd-Frank Wall Street Reform and Consumer Protection Act (the Dodd-Frank Act).

Everyone believes in and supports safe food supplies and clean air and water. But the agencies of the Federal Government have gone way beyond what was originally intended by the Congress. The hallmark feature of these regulations has been a mind-numbing complexity that minimizes the understanding of what constitutes compliance, and maximizes the opportunity for arbitrary and ad hoc bureaucratic decision-making, often through vehicles that may not be a legitimate substitute for notice-and-comment rulemaking, such as guidance and interpretive documents.

Burdensome Permitting Process. As major infrastructure projects are proposed, Federal agencies are responsible for reviewing potential impacts on safety, security, communities, and the environment. Over time, the legal requirements and processes for the permitting and review of

major infrastructure projects have developed in a siloed and ad-hoc way, creating complex processes that in some cases take multiple years to complete. Projects that are particularly large and complex, or that have significant environmental impacts, are often in the permitting and review process for several years. Up to 18 Federal agencies and 35 bureaus are responsible for individual, independent permitting and review decisions. Delays and uncertainty in project review timelines can affect critical financing and siting decisions; postpone needed upgrades, replacements, or new development; and ultimately, delay job creation and negatively affect American competitiveness. While there have been a number of efforts to improve these processes over time, they have had little quantifiable impact. Under the auspices of the infrastructure initiative, through administrative, regulatory, and legislative changes, the Administration will work to streamline and rationalize the permitting process while maintaining opportunities for meaningful public input and protecting the environment.

Highest Business Taxes in the World. The corporate tax rate in the United States is the highest in the Organization for Economic Co-operation and Development (OECD) and one of the highest in the world. While the Federal corporate income tax in the United States is 35.0 percent, after including State taxes, the rate is 38.9 percent. This compares to an average top marginal tax rate of 22.5 percent worldwide and 24.7 percent in the OECD. As long as our corporate tax rate is well above other nations, businesses will have the incentive to locate overseas, and America will continue to lose out on both jobs and tax revenue.

Low Business Investment. Due to high taxes, high regulations, and poor economic policies, real private nonresidential fixed investment has grown by only 1.3 percent each year (on a fourth quarter-over-fourth quarter basis) since 2007, compared to 4.9 percent annually before the recession. The capital stock is an important determinant of labor productivity, and weak growth in labor productivity in recent years reinforces the need for more investment.

THE HUMAN COST OF ECONOMIC STAGNATION: TOO MANY AMERICANS LEFT BEHIND

Due to the slow recovery and over-burdened job creators, American workers and their families have not seen significant gains in their wages in recent years. In 2016, real hourly wages for production workers grew by only 0.5 percent (on a December-over-December basis). From the end of 2007 to the end of 2016, real GDP grew by 12.1 percent, but real wages grew by only 7.7 percent. In 2015, 13.5 percent of Americans lived in poverty, higher than in 2007. The poverty rate among children was even higher, 19.7 percent in 2015, compared to 18 percent in 2007.

Further compounding the twin challenges of growing debt and economic stagnation are social and economic policies that have failed millions of able-bodied adults. Millions of Americans are too discouraged to remain in the labor force or are being forced to work part-time.

In December 2007, before the start of the Great Recession, the labor force participation (LFP) rate was 66.0 percent. At the end of 2016, over seven years after the end of the recession, the participation rate was 62.7 percent. This is not solely a reflection of an aging population. Even amongst "prime-age" workers (those aged 25 to 54 years), participation in the labor force has declined, from 83.1 percent at the end of 2007, to 81.5 percent at the end of 2016. For those aged 25 to 34 years, too, participation has fallen according to the U.S. Bureau of Labor Statistics (from 83.1 percent in December 2007, to 81.9 percent in December 2016). The employment-to-population ratio has fallen one percentage point for this young demographic between the end of 2007 and the end of 2016.

THE DANGEROUS COMBINATION OF HISTORIC DEBT AND ECONOMIC STAGNATION

Recent Federal budgets tell the story of a persistent and unresolved national crisis. During the Great Recession, the Federal budget deficit rose to unprecedented heights as revenue fell and spending rose sharply. From 2009 to 2012, the budget ran trillion-dollar deficits ranging in size from 6.8 percent to 9.8 percent of GDP, a standard measure of the size of deficits relative to the economy. Relative to GDP, these deficits were the largest seen since the Nation was on an all-out war footing during World War II.

From 2013 to 2016, deficits diminished from the trillion-dollar peaks, but still remained between $400 and $700 billion. These deficits were still above historical levels prior to the recession, despite coming years after the recession ended. Unless we change our fiscal course, our budget deficits will begin rising again after next year and will soon reach trillion-dollar levels once again. That would mean the publicly held debt will continue to mushroom and soon place the Nation in uncharted fiscal territory, unable to weather unexpected events such as recession or war, and vulnerable to fiscal and economic crises.

III. HOW TO MAKE THINGS RIGHT: NEW POLICIES FOR JOBS AND GROWTH AND NEW SPENDING PRIORITIES

To promote safety and prosperity for all Americans, we need to reprioritize Federal spending as we change the policies that have stifled economic growth. We need to incentivize business investment and reform the tax and regulatory systems that have been headwinds for growth. We need trade practices that will stimulate American exports and jobs. We need family friendly policies that acknowledge the reality of dual income households. In addition, we need to bring Federal deficits and debt under control so that the Federal Government no longer absorbs available capital that could go to more productive uses.

NEW POLICIES FOR JOBS AND GROWTH

The President's Budget proposes the following bold steps to spark faster economic growth, balance the budget within 10 years, and finance important new priorities.

Control Federal Spending. The first step is to bring Federal spending under control and return the Federal budget to balance within 10 years. Deficit spending has become an ingrained part of the culture in the Nation's capital. It must end to avoid passing unsustainable levels of debt on to our children and grandchildren and causing serious economic damage. When debt levels keep increasing, more and more of the Nation's resources are required to service that debt and are diverted away from Government services that citizens depend on. To help correct this and reach our budget goal in 10 years, the Budget includes $3.6 trillion in spending reductions over 10 years, the most ever proposed by any President in a Budget. By including the anticipated economic gains that will result from the President's fiscal, economic, and regulatory policies, the deficit will be reduced by $5.6 trillion compared to the current fiscal path.

As a result, by the end of the 10-year budget window, when the budget reaches balance, publicly held debt will be reduced to 60 percent of GDP, the lowest level since 2010, when the economic policies of the last administration took effect. Under this plan, the debt will continue to fall both in nominal dollars and as a share of GDP beyond that point, putting us on a path to repay the debt in full within a few decades. Bringing the budget into surplus and reducing the level of debt sets up a virtuous cycle in which fewer tax dollars are needed to service the debt. This increases budget flexibility, in which the Government can pursue other needed priorities. Reduced Federal borrowing on the capital markets also frees up capital to flow to productivity-enhancing investments, leading to higher economic growth.

The following are a few of the ways we will bring spending under control:

Repeal and Replace Obamacare. The Budget includes $250 billion in deficit savings associated with health care reform as part of the President's commitment to rescue Americans from the failures of Obamacare, and to expand choice, increase access, and lower premiums. The President supports a repeal and replace approach that improves Medicaid's sustainability and targets resources to those most in need, eliminates Obamacare's onerous taxes and mandates, provides funding for States to stabilize markets and ensure a smooth transition away from Obamacare, and helps Americans purchase the coverage they want through the use of tax credits and expanded Health Savings Accounts. Repealing Obamacare and its regulations on businesses will also increase employment, thereby increasing GDP and creating much needed economic growth. The Administration applauds the House's passage of the American Health Care Act and is committed to working with the Congress to repeal and replace Obamacare.

The Administration is committed to providing needed flexibility to issuers to help attract healthy consumers to enroll in health insurance coverage, improve the risk pool and bring stability and certainty to the individual and small group markets, while increasing the options for patients and providers. The Administration also supports State flexibility and control to create a free and open health care market and will continue to empower States to make decisions that work best for their markets. In light of these goals, the Budget promotes efficient operations and only funds critical activities for the Health Insurance Exchanges. The Administration will continue to work with the Congress to provide for a stable transition from the burdensome requirements of Obamacare and transition to a health care system focused on these core values.

Reform Medicaid. To realign financial incentives and provide stability to both Federal and State budgets, the Budget proposes to reform Medicaid by giving States the choice between a per capita cap and a block grant and empowering States to innovate and prioritize Medicaid dollars to the most vulnerable populations. States will have more flexibility to control costs and design individual, State-based solutions to provide better care to Medicaid beneficiaries. These reforms are projected to save $610 billion over 10 years.

Support the Highest Priority Biomedical Research and Development. The Budget institutes policies to ensure that Federal resources maximally support the highest priority biomedical science by reducing reimbursement of indirect costs (and thus focusing a higher percentage of spending on direct research costs) and implementing changes to the National Institutes of Health's (NIH) structure to improve efficiencies in the research enterprise. In 2018, the Department of Health and Human Services (HHS) and NIH will develop policies to reduce the burden of regulation on recipients of NIH funding consistent with the Administration's initiatives on regulatory reform and the goals articulated for the new Research Policy Board established in the 21st Century Cures Act.

Provide a Path Toward Welfare Reform. The Budget provides a path toward welfare reform, particularly to encourage those individuals dependent on the Government to return to the workforce. In doing so, this Budget includes Supplemental Nutrition Assistance Program (SNAP) reforms that tighten eligibility and encourage work, and proposals that strengthen child support and limit the Earned Income Tax Credit (EITC) and the Child Tax Credit (CTC) to those who are authorized to work in the United States.

As a primary component of the social safety net, SNAP—formerly Food Stamps—has grown significantly in the past decade. As expected, SNAP participation grew to historic

levels during the recession. However, despite improvements in unemployment since the recession ended, SNAP participation remains persistently high.

The Budget proposes a series of reforms to SNAP that close eligibility loopholes, target benefits to the neediest households, and require able-bodied adults to work. Combined, these reforms will reduce SNAP expenditures while maintaining the basic assistance low-income families need to weather hard times. The Budget also proposes SNAP reforms that will re-balance the State-Federal partnership in providing benefits by establishing a State match for benefit costs. The Budget assumes a gradual phase-in of the match, beginning with a national average of 10 percent in 2020 and increasing to an average of 25 percent by 2023. To help States manage their costs, in addition to the currently available operational choices States make that can impact participation rates and benefit calculations, new flexibilities to allow States to establish locally appropriate benefit levels will be considered.

The Budget also includes a number of proposals that strengthen the Child Support Enforcement Program, providing State agencies additional tools to create stronger, more efficient child support programs that facilitate family self-sufficiency and promote responsible parenthood. Specifically, a suite of Establishment and Enforcement proposals serves to increase child support collections that in turn result in savings to Federal benefits programs, and a Child Support Technology Fund will allow States to replace aging information technology systems to increase security, efficiency, and program integrity.

The Budget also proposes to require a Social Security Number (SSN) that is valid for work in order to claim the CTC and EITC. Under current law, individuals who do not have SSNs valid for work can claim the CTC, including the refundable portion of the credit. This proposal would ensure only people who are authorized to work in the United States are eligible for the CTC. In addition, this proposal fixes gaps in current administrative practice for EITC filers that allowed some people with SSNs that are not valid for work to still claim the EITC.

Reform Disability Programs. The Budget proposes to reform disability insurance programs to promote greater LFP. Currently, people with disabilities have low rates of LFP—20 percent—which is less than a third of the LFP rate of the overall working age population. Disability benefits are essential for workers with long-term and permanent disabilities who are unable to work. Program integrity efforts are crucial to ensure only participants who remain eligible continue receiving benefits. The greatest waste is when the Government is not doing enough to enable individuals to remain in the labor force—incentives and pathways to recover from a temporary disability and return to work. These disability insurance programs should be helping people to stay in the workforce and be self-sufficient.

At the same time, Government must ensure only those who are truly eligible receive benefits. Reform proposals in the Budget include efforts to improve program integrity, close loopholes that make the program more susceptible to fraud, and address inequities in the system. For instance, the Budget proposes to hold fraud facilitators liable for overpayments and, instead of the automatic current lifetime appointment for Federal staff reviewing applications, the Budget proposes a probationary period for all new Administrative Law Judges hired.

To test creative and effective ways to promote greater LFP of people with disabilities so individuals can be independent and self-sufficient, the Budget proposes to expand demonstration authority to allow the Administration to test new program rules and processes and require mandatory participation by program applicants and beneficiaries. An expert panel will identify specific changes to program rules that would increase LFP and reduce program participation, informed by successful demonstration results and other evidence. Past efforts have provided enhanced incentives to pursue work for disability insurance beneficiaries who already spent years out of the labor force. The Budget, in contrast, focuses on early intervention return-to-work initiatives that would help the individual worker maintain attachment to the labor force while also reducing the individuals' need to apply to the disability insurance programs.

Currently, there is a common expectation that receipt of disability benefits results in a permanent exit from the labor force. The Budget challenges this assumption by evaluating alternative program designs that will result in helping individuals with temporary work-disabilities return to work. The Budget includes targets for reduced program costs in the second five years of the budget window, savings that would result from increased LFP by people with disabilities.

Reform Federal Employees Retirement Benefits. The employee retirement landscape continues to evolve as private companies are providing less compensation in the form of retirement benefits. The shift away from defined benefit programs and cost-of-living adjustments for annuitants is part of that evolution. By comparison, the Federal Government continues to offer a very generous package of retirement benefits. Consistent with the goal of reining in Federal Government spending in many areas, as well as to bring Federal retirement benefits more in line with the private sector, adjustments to reduce the long-term costs associated with these benefits are included in this Budget. These proposals include increasing employee payments to the defined benefit Federal Employee Retirement System pension such that the employee will generally be paying the same amount as the employing agency, and reducing or eliminating cost-of-living adjustments for existing and future retirees. Viewed in the context of the broader labor environment, the Administration believes the implementation and phasing in of these changes will not impact the Federal Government's recruiting and retention efforts.

Reduce Improper Payments Government-Wide. For the past few years, improper payments have been rising, and the Budget helps fulfill the President's promise to crack down on these improper Government payments. Even though the majority of Government payments are made properly, any waste of taxpayer money is unacceptable. The Budget prioritizes shrinking the amount of improper cash out the door. Specifically, by 2027 the Budget proposes to curtail Government-wide improper payments by half through actions to improve payment accuracy and tighten administrative controls.

Reduce the Federal Government to Redefine its Proper Role and Promote Efficiency. The Budget Blueprint for 2018 provided a plan for reprioritizing Federal discretionary spending so that it advances the safety and security of the American people. It included a $54 billion increase in defense spending in 2018, which was fully offset by $54 billion in reductions to non-defense programs. The Budget provides more detail on these spending reductions and provides additional savings and reforms that are necessary to balance the budget by 2027.

Details on these spending reductions are included in a separate *Major Savings and Reforms* volume. This volume provides a specific, aggressive set of program elimination, reduction, and saving proposals that redefine the proper role of the Federal Government, and curtail programs that fall short on results or provide little return to the American people.

For instance, within HHS, in order to return the provision of social services back to State and local governments as well as the private sector, the Budget eliminates the Social Services Block Grant (SSBG), a broad-based block grant that lacks strong performance and accountability standards. Relatedly, the Budget reduces the portion of the Temporary Assistance for Needy Families (TANF) block grant (10 percent) that States may transfer from TANF to SSBG. Finally, the Budget eliminates the TANF Contingency Fund, as it fails to provide well-targeted counter-cyclical funding to States.

Redirect Foreign Aid Spending. The Budget supports the core activities of the Department of State, the U.S. Agency for International Development (USAID), and other international programs, and refocuses their work on the highest priorities and strategic objectives. These include: investing in critical embassy security and maintenance needs in order to safeguard Federal employees overseas; meeting our commitment to Israel; supporting U.S. national security in efforts to defeat the Islamic State of Iraq and Syria; preventing the spread or use of weapons of mass destruction by state or non-state actors; maintaining U.S. leadership in shaping global humanitarian assistance while also asking the rest of the world to increase their share; fostering opportunities for U.S. economic interests by combatting corruption and ensuring a level playing field for American businesses; advancing global health security and pandemic preparedness; and ensuring effectiveness and accountability to the U.S. taxpayer. The Budget will also continue to support ongoing commitments to global health programs, including completing our commitment to Gavi, the Vaccine Alliance, maintaining funding for malaria programs, and continuing treatment for all current HIV/AIDS patients under the U.S. President's Emergency Plan for Aids Relief.

The Budget proposes to reduce or end direct funding for international programs and organizations whose missions do not substantially advance U.S. foreign policy interests. The Budget also renews attention on the appropriate U.S. share of international spending at the United Nations, at the World Bank, and for many other global issues where the United States currently pays more than its fair share. In addition, this Budget request focuses on making the Department of State and USAID leaner, more efficient, and more effective, and streamlines international affairs agencies more broadly through the elimination of Federal funding to several smaller agencies. The Budget will allow the Department of State and USAID to support their core missions, while ensuring the best use of American taxpayer dollars in ways that advance national security as we work to build a more prosperous and peaceful world.

Reduce Non-Defense Discretionary Spending Each Year with a 2-Penny Plan. The Budget Blueprint outlined a plan to reduce non-defense discretionary spending by $54 billion in 2018. As part of the plan to achieve a balanced budget by 2027, the Budget builds on this approach with a 2-penny plan that would reduce non-defense budget authority by two percent each year, to reach approximately $385 billion in 2027, or just over 1.2 percent of GDP. For comparison, at the 2017 cap level, non-defense base budget authority is $519 billion and 2.7 percent of GDP. This reduction may seem steep, but the strict and disciplined discretionary policies already proposed in the Budget Blueprint will serve as a down payment on the out-year reforms the Administration will unveil, as it seeks to downsize the mission of the non-defense discretionary budget in the coming years.

Simplify the Tax Code and Provide Tax Relief. A comprehensive overhaul to our tax code will boost economic growth and investment. A simpler, fairer, and more efficient tax system is critical to growing the economy and creating jobs. Our outdated, overly complex, and burdensome tax system must be reformed to unleash America's economy, and create millions of new, better-paying jobs that enable American workers to meet their families' needs.

The Budget assumes deficit neutral tax reform, which the Administration will work closely with the Congress to enact.

The Administration has articulated several core principles that will guide its discussions with taxpayers, businesses, Members of Congress, and other stakeholders. Overall, the Administration believes that tax reform, both for individuals and businesses, should grow the economy and make America a more attractive business environment.

Tax relief for American families, especially middle-income families, should:

- Lower individual income tax rates.

- Expand the standard deduction and help families struggling with child and dependent care expenses.

- Protect homeownership, charitable giving and retirement saving.

- End the burdensome alternative minimum tax, which requires many taxpayers to calculate their taxes twice.

- Repeal the 3.8 percent Obamacare surcharge on capital gains and dividends, which further hinders capital formation.

- And, abolish the death tax, which penalizes farmers and small business owners who want to pass their family enterprises on to their children.

The Administration believes that business tax reform should:

- Reduce the tax rate on American businesses in order to fuel job creation and economic growth.

- Eliminate most special interest tax breaks to make the tax code more equitable, **more** efficient, and to help pay for lower business tax rates.

- And, end the penalty on American business-es by transitioning to a territorial system of taxation, enabling these businesses to repa-triate their newly earned overseas profits without incurring additional taxes. This transition would include a one-time repatri-ation tax on already accumulated overseas income.

Going forward, the President is committed to continue working with the Congress and other stakeholders to carefully and deliberatively build on these principles to create a tax system that is fair, simple, and efficient—one that puts Americans back to work and puts America first.

Provide a Comprehensive Plan to Reform the Federal Government and Reduce the Federal Civilian Workforce. During the first 100 days of this Administration, the Office of Management and Budget issued guidance that takes steps to implement the President's charge to reorganize agencies and reduce the Federal workforce to begin the work of creating a leaner, more accountable, less intrusive, and more ef-fective Government. Each executive department and agency will be examined and the American public will have an opportunity to provide input. The result will be a comprehensive Government reform plan that eliminates unnecessary, over-lapping, outdated and ineffective programs. Some agencies may find the greatest efficiencies come from insourcing or reducing management layers while others will want to review pro-grams, shared service and outsourcing options, or restructuring. This may mean reorganizing, consolidating, and eliminating programs, func-tions, and organizations where necessary.

Rather than setting arbitrary targets, the Administration tasked each agency to deter-mine workforce levels that align with effectively and efficiently delivering its mission, including planning for funding levels in the President's Budget. In addition to broad agency reform, the Administration is committed to removing the

red tape that often traps Federal employees in an overly bureaucratic environment. It is often heard that managers are unable to function at an optimal level, given unnecessary layers of disjointed guidance, policy, and regulation. To alleviate this barrier to managing an efficient and effective workforce, a standard requirement included in the Agency Reform plan response is a plan for how agencies will reward top performers, while holding those with conduct or performance issues accountable.

Roll Back Burdensome Regulations. The American people deserve a regulatory system that works for them, not against them—a sys-tem that is both effective and efficient. Each year, however, Federal agencies issue thousands of new regulations that, taken together, impose substantial burdens on American consumers and businesses big and small. These burdens function much like taxes that unnecessarily inhibit growth and employment. The President is committed to fixing these problems by elimi-nating unnecessary and wasteful regulations. To that end, the President has already taken four significant steps:

Launch a Regulatory Freeze. On January 20, 2017, the President's Chief of Staff issued a memorandum to all agencies, directing them to pull back any regulations that had been sent to, but not yet published by, the Office of the Federal Register; to not publish any new regulations unless approved by one of the President's political appointees; and to delay the effective date of any pend-ing regulations for 60 days to provide the new Administration time to review and re-consider those regulations. Federal agencies responded by pulling back over 60 so-called "midnight" regulations from being issued and continue to take a very close look at those published, but not yet in effect.

Control Costs and Eliminate Unnecessary Regulations. On January 30, 2017, the President signed Executive Order (EO) 13771, "Reducing Regulation and Controlling Regulatory Costs." This EO emphasizes a critical principle for the regulatory state. It requires Federal agencies to identify for elimination at least two existing regulations for each new regulation they issue. It generally also requires agencies to ensure that for 2017, the total incremental cost of all new regulations be no greater than $0. For 2018 and beyond, the EO establishes and institutionalizes a disciplined process for imposing regulatory cost caps and allowances for each Federal agency.

Establish Executive Order (EO) 13777, "Enforcing the Regulatory Reform Agenda." This EO establishes within each agency a Regulatory Reform Officer and a Regulatory Reform Task Force to carry out the President's regulatory reform priorities. These new teams will work hard to identify regulations that eliminate jobs or inhibit job creation; are outdated, unnecessary, or ineffective; or impose costs that exceed benefits. These efforts build upon a widely recognized and bipartisan consensus that many existing regulations are likely to be ineffective and no longer necessary. The difference, however, is accountability, and these teams and this effort will be a critical means by which Federal agencies will identify and cut regulations in a smart and efficient manner.

Reform Financial Regulation and Prevent Taxpayer-Funded Bailouts. The Budget fosters economic growth and vibrant financial markets by rolling back the regulatory excesses mandated by the Dodd-Frank Act. On February 3, 2017, the Administration issued an EO on Core Principles for Regulating the United States Financial System (Core Principles EO), which includes preventing taxpayer-funded bailouts and restoring accountability within Federal financial regulatory agencies.

As directed in the Core Principles EO, the Secretary of the Treasury, with the heads of the member agencies of the Financial Stability Oversight Council, is conducting a thorough review of the extent to which existing laws,

regulations, and other Government policies promote (or inhibit) these Core Principles. The Budget includes $35 billion in savings to be realized through reforms that prevent bailouts and reverse burdensome regulations that hinder financial innovation and reduce access to credit for hardworking American families.

Further, the Budget proposes legislation to restructure the Consumer Financial Protection Bureau (CFPB). CFPB's interpretation of the Dodd-Frank Act has resulted in an unaccountable bureaucracy controlled by an independent director with unchecked regulatory authority and punitive power. Restructuring is required to ensure appropriate congressional oversight and to refocus CFPB's efforts on enforcing the law rather than impeding free commerce. The Budget proposes to limit CFPB's funding in 2018 to allow for an efficient transition period and bring a newly streamlined agency into the regular appropriations process beginning in 2019.

The Budget also proposes to restore the Securities and Exchange Commission's accountability to the American taxpayer by eliminating the "Reserve Fund" created by the Dodd-Frank Act.

Reform Immigration Policy. America's immigration policy must serve our national interest. The Budget supports commonsense immigration standards that protect American workers, reduce burdens on taxpayers and public resources, and focus Federal funds on underserved and disadvantaged citizens. When fully implemented, these changes have the potential to save American taxpayers trillions of dollars over future decades.

Census data show that current U.S. immigration policy results in a large numbers of residents and citizens who struggle to become financially independent and instead rely on Government benefits financed by taxpayers. In 2012, the census reported that 51 percent of all households headed by immigrants received payments from at least one welfare or low-income assistance program. In addition, participation in welfare programs among immigrant-headed households varies by education level. In 2012, 76 percent of households headed by an immigrant without a high school education used at least one major welfare program compared to 26 percent for households headed by an immigrant with at least a bachelor's degree. Focusing immigration policy on merit-based admissions has the potential to reduce Federal outlays for welfare payments to lower-skilled immigrant-headed households.

Estimates from a recent report by the National Academy of Sciences (NAS) on the Economic and Fiscal Consequences of Immigration indicate that each individual immigrant who lacks a high school education may create as much as $247,000 more in costs at all levels of government than they pay in taxes over the next 75 years. Based on data from the Census Bureau's Current Population Survey, 8.2 million adults with a high school education or less settled in the United States from abroad between 2000 and 2015.

The NAS study also found that, in 2013, first-generation immigrants (across all skill levels) and their dependents living in the United States may have cost government at all levels as much as $279 billion more than they paid in taxes for all levels of government, when the costs of national defense and other public goods are included on an average cost basis. The Federal costs alone were estimated to be as much as $147 billion if all public goods and benefits are included.

Some of this cost is driven by our Nation's current refugee policy. Under the refugee program, the Federal Government brings tens of thousands of entrants into the United States, on top of existing legal immigration flows, who are instantly eligible for time-limited cash benefits and numerous non-cash Federal benefits, including food assistance through SNAP, medical care, and education, as well as a host of State and local benefits.

A large proportion of entrants arriving as refugees have minimal levels of education, presenting particular fiscal costs. The HHS Annual Survey of Refugees showed that, in 2015, those who had arrived in the previous five years had less than 10 years of education on average. The survey also showed that of refugees who arrived in the prior five years nearly 50 percent were on Medicaid in 2015, 45 percent received cash assistance, and 75 percent received benefits from SNAP. These federally supported benefit programs are not tracked separately in terms of welfare and other benefits; they are added to the bottom line of the Federal deficit and Federal programs. The way that refugee spending is typically budgeted for makes it difficult to attribute the full fiscal costs, including appropriated funds for the Department of State and HHS, along with fee-funded programs from the Department of Homeland Security. Additional State and local funding for services, including public education, is not captured in the Federal budget, nor are local and State taxes collected from refugees to the Federal Government. While HHS is appropriated funds specifically for refugee benefits, many others, including SNAP and Medicaid, are unallocated to refugees.

The paradoxical effect of refugee spending is that the larger the number the United States admits for domestic resettlement, the fewer people the United States is able to help overall; each refugee admitted into the United States comes at the expense of helping a potentially greater number out of country. Thus, reducing the number of refugees increases the number of dislocated persons the United States is financially able to assist, while increasing the number of refugees may have the effect of reducing the total size of the refugee population the United States is able to assist financially.

The Administration is exploring options for budget presentation that would make transparent the net budgetary effects of immigration programs and policy. The goal of such changes would be to capture better the impact of immigration policy decisions on the Federal Government's fiscal path. Once the net effect of immigration on the Federal Budget is more clearly illustrated, the American public can be better informed about options for improving policy outcomes and saving taxpayer resources. In that regard, the Budget supports reforming the U.S. immigration system to encourage: merit-based admissions for legal immigrants, ending the entry of illegal immigrants, and a substantial reduction in refugees slotted for domestic resettlement.

NEW PRIORITIES

The Budget reprioritizes spending in several important ways.

Invest in Defense. The President's Budget includes $639 billion of discretionary budget authority for the Department of Defense (DOD), a $52 billion increase above the 2017 annualized continuing resolution (CR) level, fully offset by targeted reductions elsewhere. These resources provide for the military forces needed to conduct ongoing operations, deter potential adversaries, and protect the security of the United States.

Reverse the Defense Sequestration. The Budget fully reverses the defense sequestration by increasing funding for national defense by $54 billion above the cap in current law, and fully offsetting this increase. This includes a $52 billion increase for the DOD, as well as $2 billion of increases for other national defense programs. Since defense sequestration was first triggered in 2013, the world has grown more dangerous due to rising terrorism, destabilizing technology, and increasingly aggressive potential adversaries. Over the same period, our military has become smaller, and deferred training, maintenance, and modernization have degraded its ability to prepare for future war while sustaining current operations. The President's Budget ends this depletion and begins to rebuild the U.S. Armed Forces, laying the groundwork for a larger, more capable, and more lethal joint force consistent with a new National Defense Strategy.

Fill Critical Gaps and Build Warfighting Readiness. The Administration inherited the smallest Army since before World War II, a Navy and Marine Corps facing shortfalls in maintenance and equipment procurement, and the smallest Air Force with the oldest planes in history. The President began corrective action immediately, ordering a readiness review, requesting $30 billion of additional 2017 appropriations (of which the Congress provided $21 billion), and developing a budget that adds $54 billion to national defense in 2018. These funds will begin years of increased investment to end the depletion of our military and build warfighting readiness. In 2018, the Budget provides for 56,400 more Soldiers, Sailors, Airmen, and Marines than the end strength planned by the Obama Administration. These troops are needed to fill gaps in our combat formations, man essential units previously scheduled for divestment, and provide critical enablers. The Budget prioritizes readiness, funding critical shipyard requirements, accelerating depot maintenance and weapon system sustainment, enhancing training, growing our cyber workforce and capabilities, and restoring degraded infrastructure. Funds also recapitalize, modernize, and enhance weapons systems. For example, the Air Force, Navy, and Marine Corps would buy 84 new fighter aircraft in 2018, including 70 Joint Strike Fighters and 14 Super Hornets. The Navy continues to increase its ship count, with the acquisition of eight new battle force ships funded in 2018.

Implement Defense Reform. The Budget lays the groundwork for an ambitious reform agenda that underscores the President's commitment to reduce the costs of military programs wherever feasible without reducing effectiveness or efficiency. The Budget also continues ongoing efforts to improve the Department's business processes, reduce major headquarters activities by 25 percent, and eliminate redundant spending on service contracts.

Increase Border Security and Investments in Public Safety. The President's Budget includes $44.1 billion for the Department of Homeland Security (DHS) and $27.7 billion for the Department of Justice (DOJ) for law enforcement, public safety and immigration enforcement programs and activities.

Increase Border Security Infrastructure and Technology. The President's Budget secures the borders of the United States by investing $2.6 billion in high-priority tactical infrastructure and border security technology, including funding to plan, design, and construct a physical wall along the southern border as directed by the President's January 25, 2017 EO. This investment would strengthen border security, helping stem the flow of people, drugs, and other illicit material illegally crossing the border.

Increase DHS Personnel. The Budget also advances the President's plan to strengthen border security and immigration enforcement with more than $300 million to recruit, hire, and train 500 new Border Patrol Agents and 1,000 new Immigration and Customs Enforcement law enforcement personnel in 2018, plus associated support staff. These new personnel would improve the integrity of the immigration system by adding capacity to interdict those aliens attempting to cross the border illegally, as well as to identify and remove those already in the United States who entered illegally.

Enforce the Nation's Laws. The Budget enhances enforcement of immigration laws by proposing an additional $1.5 billion above the 2017 annualized CR level for expanded detention, transportation, and removal of illegal immigrants. These funds would ensure that DHS has sufficient detention capacity to hold prioritized aliens, including violent criminals and other dangerous individuals, as they are processed for removal.

Invest in Law Enforcement. The Budget provides critical resources for DOJ to confront terrorism, reduce violent crime, tackle the Nation's opioid epidemic, and combat illegal immigration. Additional spending is provided for DOJ to enhance public safety and law enforcement including $214 million above current levels for immigration enforcement—allowing DOJ to hire 75 additional immigration judge teams, bringing the total number of funded immigration judge teams to 449. In addition, $84 million more is provided for increases in the Federal detainee population. Increases of $188 million are included to address violent and gun-related crime in communities across the Nation and to target transnational criminal organizations and drug traffickers. As part of this increase, $103 million is added to maintain and expand capacity to fight against opioids and other illicit drugs. Further, DOJ will take steps to mitigate the risk that sanctuary jurisdictions pose to public safety.

Invest in Cybersecurity. The internet has transformed and modernized our society and enabled astonishing business growth. It has fostered education, fueled innovation, and strengthened our military. That transformation—and the opportunities it has created—has been exploited by our enemies and adversaries. Bad actors must not be allowed to use the internet to perpetrate crimes and threaten our security. These crimes affect our largest companies, impact millions of people at a time, damage our small businesses, and affect our national security. The Budget supports the President's focus on cybersecurity to ensure strong programs and technology to defend the Federal networks that serve the American people, and continues efforts to share information, standards, and best practices with critical infrastructure and American businesses to keep them secure. The Budget also includes an increase in law enforcement and cybersecurity personnel across DHS, DOD, and the Federal Bureau of Investigation to execute these efforts and counter cybercrime. In addition, the Budget includes an increase in resources for the National Cybersecurity and

Communications Integration Center, which enables DHS to respond effectively to cyber attacks on critical infrastructure.

Provide an Infrastructure Plan to Support $1 Trillion in Private/Public Infrastructure Investment. The President has consistently emphasized that the Nation's infrastructure needs to be rebuilt and modernized to create jobs, maintain America's economic competitiveness, and connect communities and people to more opportunities. Unfortunately, the United States no longer has the best infrastructure in the world. According to the World Economic Forum, the United States' overall infrastructure places 12th, with countries such as Japan, Germany, the Netherlands, and France ranking higher.

If the United States continues to underinvest in infrastructure, we will continue to fall further and further behind our peers and our economic performance will suffer. Given these challenges, the Administration's goal is to seek long-term reforms on how infrastructure projects are regulated, funded, delivered, and maintained. Simply providing more Federal funding for infrastructure is not the solution. Rather, we will work to fix underlying incentives, procedures, and policies to spur better, and more efficient, infrastructure decisions and outcomes, across a range of sectors, including surface transportation, airports, waterways, ports, drinking and waste water, broadband and key Federal facilities. Such improvements will include tracking the progress of major infrastructure projects on a public dashboard to ensure transparency and accountability of the permitting process.

The President's target of $1 trillion will be met with a combination of new Federal funding, incentivized non-Federal funding, and expedited projects that would not have happened but for the Administration's involvement (for example, the Keystone XL Pipeline). While the Administration will propose additional funding for infrastructure, those funds will be focused on incentivizing additional non-Federal investments. While the Administration continues to work with the Congress, States, localities, and other infrastructure stakeholders to finalize the suite of direct Federal programs that will support this effort, the Budget includes $200 billion in outlays related to the infrastructure initiative.

The impact of this investment will be amplified with other administrative and regulatory actions the Administration plans to pursue. The Administration is comprehensively reviewing administrative policies that impact infrastructure, and will eliminate and revise policies that no longer fulfill a useful purpose. Further, as part of the regulatory reform agenda, the Administration will eliminate or significantly revise regulations that create unnecessary barriers to infrastructure investment by all levels of government and the private sector.

The United States has maintained an excellent aviation safety record while operating the world's most congested airspace. Despite this record, the Federal Aviation Administration (FAA) is challenged increasingly to address the quickly evolving needs of the Nation's airspace users.

To accommodate growing air traffic volume and meet the demands of aviation users, the Administration proposes to shift the air traffic control functions to a non-profit, non-governmental entity. Similar efforts have been undertaken successfully in many other countries. This transformative undertaking will create an innovative corporation that can more nimbly respond to the demand for air traffic services, all while reducing taxes and Government spending. The parts of FAA that will remain with the Government will retain important aviation safety regulatory activities as well as maintain the Airport Improvement Program grant program.

The Budget reflects the proposal to shift the air traffic control function to an independent, non-governmental organization beginning in 2021, with a cap reduction in discretionary spending of $72.8 billion, and reduction in aviation excise taxes of $115.6 billion. These estimated changes represent a high-level reflection of the Administration's proposal.

Support Families and Children. The Administration is committed to helping American families and children.

Provide Paid Parental Leave. During his campaign, the President pledged to provide paid family leave to help new parents. The Budget delivers on this promise with a fully paid-for proposal to provide six weeks of paid family leave to new mothers and fathers, including adoptive parents, so all families can afford to take time to recover from childbirth and bond with a new child without worrying about paying their bills.

Using the Unemployment Insurance (UI) system as a base, the proposal will allow States to establish paid parental leave programs in a way that is most appropriate for their workforce and economy. States would be required to provide six weeks of parental leave and the proposal gives States broad latitude to design and finance the program. The proposal is fully offset by a package of sensible reforms to the UI system—including reforms to reduce improper payments, help unemployed workers find jobs more quickly, and encourage States to maintain reserves in their Unemployment Trust Fund accounts. The Administration looks forward to working with the Congress on legislation to make paid parental leave a reality for families across the Nation.

Extend the Children's Health Insurance Program (CHIP). While the future of CHIP is addressed alongside other health reforms, the Budget proposes to extend CHIP funding for two years, through 2019, providing stability to States and families. The Budget also proposes a series of improvements that rebalance the State-Federal partnership, including returning to the historic Federal matching rate, and increasing State flexibility.

Reform Student Loan Programs. In recent years, income-driven repayment (IDR) plans, which offer student borrowers the option of making affordable monthly payments based on factors such as income and family size, have grown in popularity. However, the numerous IDR plans currently offered to borrowers overly complicate choosing and enrolling in the right plan. The Budget proposes to streamline student loan repayment by consolidating multiple IDR plans into a single plan. The single IDR plan would cap a borrower's monthly payment at 12.5 percent of discretionary income. For undergraduate borrowers, any balance remaining after 15 years of repayment would be forgiven. For borrowers with any graduate debt, any balance remaining after 30 years of repayment would be forgiven.

To support this streamlined pathway to debt relief for undergraduate borrowers, and to generate savings that help put the Nation on a more sustainable fiscal path, the Budget eliminates the Public Service Loan Forgiveness program, establishes reforms to guarantee that all borrowers in IDR pay an equitable share of their income, and eliminates subsidized loans. These reforms will reduce inefficiencies in the student loan program and focus assistance on needy undergraduate student borrowers instead of high-income, high-balance graduate borrowers. All student loan proposals apply to loans originated on or after July 1, 2018, except those provided to borrowers to finish their current course of study.

The Budget also supports expanded access to Pell Grants for eligible recipients through Year-Round Pell. This policy incentivizes students to complete their degrees faster, helping them reduce their loan debt and enter the workforce sooner. Year-Round Pell gives students the opportunity to earn a third semester of Pell Grant support during an academic year, boosting total Pell Grant aid by $1.5 billion in 2018 for approximately 900,000 students.

Extend the Current VA Choice Program. Veterans' access to timely, high quality health care is one of this Administration's highest priorities. The Budget provides mandatory funding to extend the Veterans Choice Program, enabling eligible veterans to receive timely care, close to home. As of April 2017, veterans have completed over 8.7 million appointments through the Choice Program. The Administration will work with the Congress to improve this program and implement bold change so that the Department of Veterans Affairs (VA) continues to provide the services and choices veterans have earned. The Budget proposes to fully offset the cost of continuing this program through targeted programmatic changes to mandatory benefits programs to better align them with programmatic intents. Through these tradeoffs, VA will focus its budgetary resources on providing veterans with the most efficient and effective care and benefits.

Summary Tables

Table S–1. Budget Totals

(In billions of dollars and as a percent of GDP)

	2016	2017	2018	2019	2020	2021	2022	2023	2024	2025	2026	2027	Totals 2018-2022	Totals 2018-2027
Budget Totals in Billions of Dollars:														
Receipts	3,268	3,460	3,654	3,814	3,982	4,161	4,390	4,615	4,864	5,130	5,417	5,724	20,001	45,751
Outlays	3,853	4,062	4,094	4,340	4,470	4,617	4,832	4,933	5,073	5,306	5,527	5,708	22,353	48,901
Deficit/surplus (–)	585	603	440	526	488	456	442	319	209	176	110	-16	2,351	3,150
Debt held by the public	14,168	14,824	15,353	15,957	16,509	17,024	17,517	17,887	18,150	18,379	18,541	18,575		
Gross domestic product (GDP)	18,407	19,162	20,014	20,947	21,981	23,093	24,261	25,489	26,779	28,134	29,557	31,053		
Budget Totals as a Percent of GDP:														
Receipts	17.8%	18.1%	18.3%	18.2%	18.1%	18.0%	18.1%	18.1%	18.2%	18.2%	18.3%	18.4%	18.1%	18.2%
Outlays	20.9%	21.2%	20.5%	20.7%	20.3%	20.0%	19.9%	19.4%	18.9%	18.9%	18.7%	18.4%	20.3%	19.6%
Deficit/surplus (–)	3.2%	3.1%	2.2%	2.5%	2.2%	2.0%	1.8%	1.3%	0.8%	0.6%	0.4%	-0.1%	2.1%	1.4%
Debt held by the public	77.0%	77.4%	76.7%	76.2%	75.1%	73.7%	72.2%	70.2%	67.8%	65.3%	62.7%	59.8%		

Table S–2. Effect of Budget Proposals on Projected Deficits

(Deficit increases (+) or decreases (-) in billions of dollars)

	2016	2017	2018	2019	2020	2021	2022	2023	2024	2025	2026	2027	Totals 2018-2022	Totals 2018-2027
Projected deficits in the pre-policy baseline	585	605	413	553	647	743	881	925	956	1,082	1,234	1,338	3,238	8,775
Percent of GDP	3.2%	3.2%	2.1%	2.7%	3.0%	3.3%	3.8%	3.8%	3.8%	4.1%	4.5%	4.7%		
Proposals in the 2018 Budget:														
Major initiatives:														
Repeal and replace Obamacare			25	30	-5	-30	-35	-40	-40	-50	-50	-55	-15	-250
Support $1 trillion in private/public infrastructure investment			5	25	40	50	40	20	10	5	5	....	160	200
Reform financial regulation and prevent taxpayer-funded bailouts				-2	-3	-3	-4	-4	-4	-4	-4	-5	-13	-35
Establish a paid parental leave program			1	1	2	2	2	2	2	2	2	2	7	19
Reform Medicaid and the Children's Health Insurance Program (CHIP)			-2	-3	-10	-20	-40	-60	-80	-105	-130	-165	-76	-616
Reform the welfare system			-9	-16	-23	-25	-30	-33	-33	-34	-35	-34	-102	-272
Reform Federal student loans			-4	-7	-11	-13	-15	-17	-18	-19	-19	-20	-50	-143
Reduce improper payments Government-wide			-0	-1	-2	-3	-5	-5	-10	-21	-38	-58	-10	-142
Reform disability programs			-1	-1	-2	-2	-3	-5	-8	-12	-17	-22	-9	-72
Reform retirement benefits for Federal employees			-4	-1	-3	-4	-6	-7	-8	-9	-10	-11	-17	-63
Limit Farm Bill subsidies and make other agricultural reforms			-*	-3	-4	-4	-4	-4	-4	-5	-5	-5	-15	-38
Extend the current Veterans Choice program			1	2	2	3	3	4	4	4	4	4	11	29
Other spending reductions and program reforms			-7	-12	-16	-17	-26	-35	-38	-27	-71	-89	-79	-339
Total, major initiatives			4	10	-32	-67	-122	-185	-228	-276	-369	-458	-208	-1,723
Reprioritize discretionary spending:														
Eliminate the defense sequester and raise the cap on defense discretionary spending		2	42	52	52	50	49	48	47	45	43	41	245	469
Reorganize Government and apply two-penny plan to non-defense discretionary spending		-5	-15	-49	-81	-112	-133	-156	-179	-202	-226	-251	-390	-1,404
Phase down the use of Overseas Contingency Operations funding[1]		1	-2	-16	-33	-51	-69	-77	-82	-85	-87	-90	-171	-593
Total, reprioritize discretionary spending		-3	25	-13	-63	-113	-152	-185	-214	-243	-271	-299	-316	-1,528
Debt service and indirect interest effects		-*	*	*	-1	-5	-12	-24	-38	-55	-76	-101	-18	-311
Total proposals in the 2018 Budget		-3	29	-3	-96	-185	-287	-394	-480	-573	-715	-858	-542	-3,563
Effect of economic feedback		*	-2	-24	-63	-102	-153	-213	-267	-333	-408	-496	-345	-2,062
Total deficit reduction in the 2018 Budget		-3	27	-28	-159	-288	-440	-607	-747	-906	-1,124	-1,354	-887	-5,625
Resulting deficit/surplus (-) in the 2018 Budget	585	603	440	526	488	456	442	319	209	176	110	-16	2,351	3,150
Percent of GDP	3.2%	3.1%	2.2%	2.5%	2.2%	2.0%	1.8%	1.3%	0.8%	0.6%	0.4%	-0.1%		

* $500 million or less

[1] Reductions associated with OCO are relative to the BBEDCA baseline and are based on notional placeholder amounts that are consistent with a potential transition of certain OCO costs into the base budget while continuing to fund contingency operations. The placeholder amounts do not reflect specific decisions or assumptions about OCO funding in any particular year.

Table S–3. Baseline by Category [1]

(In billions of dollars)

	2016	2017	2018	2019	2020	2021	2022	2023	2024	2025	2026	2027	Totals 2018-2022	Totals 2018-2027
Outlays:														
Discretionary programs:														
Defense	585	592	600	623	640	653	665	676	695	713	732	750	3,181	6,747
Non-defense	600	624	618	629	637	650	659	672	688	705	722	739	3,193	6,718
Subtotal, discretionary programs	1,185	1,215	1,219	1,251	1,277	1,303	1,323	1,348	1,384	1,418	1,453	1,488	6,373	13,464
Mandatory programs:														
Social Security	910	946	1,005	1,070	1,138	1,207	1,281	1,362	1,448	1,537	1,630	1,728	5,702	13,406
Medicare	588	593	582	646	701	757	854	885	913	1,012	1,106	1,195	3,541	8,650
Medicaid	368	378	408	432	454	480	507	537	570	604	648	688	2,280	5,328
Other mandatory programs	560	656	589	626	643	670	717	719	726	759	821	846	3,244	7,115
Subtotal, mandatory programs	2,427	2,573	2,583	2,774	2,936	3,114	3,359	3,503	3,656	3,912	4,205	4,457	14,767	34,500
Net interest	240	276	316	372	431	487	542	592	634	670	706	741	2,147	5,489
Total outlays	3,853	4,065	4,118	4,398	4,643	4,905	5,224	5,443	5,673	6,000	6,364	6,687	23,287	53,453
Receipts:														
Individual income taxes	1,546	1,660	1,836	1,934	2,042	2,165	2,291	2,425	2,568	2,719	2,880	3,058	10,268	23,918
Corporation income taxes	300	324	355	375	401	400	414	425	439	455	475	497	1,945	4,235
Social insurance and retirement receipts:														
Social Security payroll taxes	810	857	892	931	972	1,027	1,081	1,133	1,191	1,251	1,316	1,379	4,903	11,173
Medicare payroll taxes	247	258	270	283	297	315	332	348	367	386	407	427	1,497	3,432
Unemployment insurance	49	49	50	49	49	50	51	52	53	54	56	57	248	519
Other retirement	9	10	10	11	11	12	12	13	13	14	15	16	56	127
Excise taxes	95	87	106	107	110	114	116	119	123	127	131	136	553	1,189
Estate and gift taxes	21	23	24	26	28	29	31	33	36	38	40	43	139	328
Customs duties	35	34	40	42	43	44	46	50	53	56	60	65	214	499
Deposits of earnings, Federal Reserve System	116	97	70	56	49	51	60	70	78	86	91	98	286	709
Other miscellaneous receipts	40	60	54	56	57	58	60	61	64	65	67	69	284	610
Total receipts	3,268	3,460	3,707	3,869	4,059	4,264	4,495	4,730	4,984	5,251	5,538	5,844	20,394	46,741
Deficit	585	605	411	529	584	641	728	713	689	749	826	842	2,894	6,712
Net interest	240	276	316	372	431	487	542	592	634	670	706	741	2,147	5,489
Primary deficit	345	329	95	157	153	154	187	121	55	79	120	101	746	1,224
On-budget deficit	620	647	436	533	564	612	682	640	593	627	681	668	2,826	6,035
Off-budget deficit/surplus (−)	−36	−42	−25	−4	20	29	47	72	97	122	145	174	68	678

Table S–3. Baseline by Category[1]—Continued

(In billions of dollars)

	2016	2017	2018	2019	2020	2021	2022	2023	2024	2025	2026	2027	Totals 2018-2022	Totals 2018-2027
Memorandum, budget authority for discretionary programs:														
Defense	607	616	616	630	645	661	677	694	711	729	747	765	3,229	6,875
Non-defense	560	551	548	562	575	589	604	619	634	650	667	683	2,879	6,133
Total, discretionary budget authority	1,167	1,167	1,164	1,192	1,221	1,250	1,281	1,313	1,346	1,379	1,414	1,449	6,108	13,008
Memorandum, totals with pre-policy economic assumptions:														
Receipts	3,268	3,467	3,707	3,838	3,991	4,151	4,330	4,505	4,703	4,902	5,116	5,339	20,017	44,581
Outlays	3,853	4,072	4,120	4,392	4,638	4,894	5,211	5,431	5,659	5,984	6,350	6,678	23,255	53,356
Deficit	585	605	413	553	647	743	881	925	956	1,082	1,234	1,338	3,238	8,775

[1] Baseline estimates are on the basis of the economic assumptions shown in Table S-9, which incorporate the effects of the Administration's fiscal policies. Baseline totals reflecting current-law economic assumptions are shown in a memorandum bank.

Table S–4. Proposed Budget by Category
(In billions of dollars)

	2016	2017	2018	2019	2020	2021	2022	2023	2024	2025	2026	2027	Totals 2018-2022	Totals 2018-2027
Outlays:														
Discretionary programs:														
Defense	585	594	643	665	670	667	662	665	679	693	708	722	3,307	6,774
Non-defense	600	619	601	567	537	506	485	464	455	446	437	429	2,696	4,927
Subtotal, discretionary programs	1,185	1,213	1,244	1,232	1,207	1,173	1,148	1,129	1,134	1,139	1,145	1,151	6,003	11,701
Mandatory programs:														
Social Security	910	946	1,005	1,070	1,137	1,205	1,279	1,360	1,446	1,535	1,628	1,725	5,696	13,392
Medicare	588	593	582	646	700	756	851	882	910	1,017	1,085	1,166	3,535	8,594
Medicaid	368	378	404	423	439	460	467	477	490	499	518	524	2,193	4,701
Other mandatory programs	560	656	570	603	609	622	658	653	649	667	687	678	3,062	6,396
Allowance for Obamacare repeal and replacement	....	....	–30	–30	–90	–130	–140	–155	–160	–170	–170	–175	–420	–1,250
Allowance for infrastructure initiative	....	....	5	25	40	50	40	20	10	5	5	....	160	200
Subtotal, mandatory programs	2,427	2,573	2,535	2,736	2,835	2,963	3,156	3,237	3,345	3,553	3,754	3,919	14,226	32,033
Net interest	240	276	315	371	428	481	528	567	595	613	629	639	2,123	5,166
Total outlays	3,853	4,062	4,094	4,340	4,470	4,617	4,832	4,933	5,073	5,306	5,527	5,708	22,353	48,901
Receipts:														
Individual income taxes	1,546	1,660	1,836	1,935	2,044	2,167	2,293	2,428	2,572	2,723	2,884	3,062	10,275	23,945
Corporation income taxes	300	324	355	375	401	400	414	425	439	455	475	497	1,946	4,236
Social insurance and retirement receipts:														
Social Security payroll taxes	810	857	892	931	972	1,027	1,081	1,133	1,191	1,251	1,316	1,379	4,903	11,173
Medicare payroll taxes	247	258	270	283	297	315	332	348	367	386	407	427	1,497	3,432
Unemployment insurance	49	49	50	49	50	53	55	54	56	56	59	62	257	543
Other retirement	9	10	12	14	16	18	20	22	23	24	25	26	80	199
Excise taxes	95	87	106	107	110	99	101	104	106	109	113	117	524	1,072
Estate and gift taxes	21	23	24	26	28	29	31	33	36	38	40	43	139	328
Customs duties	35	34	40	42	43	44	46	50	53	56	60	65	214	499
Deposits of earnings, Federal Reserve System	116	97	70	56	50	52	61	71	78	87	92	99	290	717
Other miscellaneous receipts	40	60	54	55	57	57	59	61	63	64	66	69	282	606
Allowance for Obamacare repeal and replacement	....	....	–55	–60	–85	–100	–105	–115	–120	–120	–120	–120	–405	–1,000
Total receipts	3,268	3,460	3,654	3,814	3,982	4,161	4,390	4,615	4,864	5,130	5,417	5,724	20,001	45,751
Deficit/surplus (–)	585	603	440	526	488	456	442	319	209	176	110	–16	2,351	3,150
Net interest	240	276	315	371	428	481	528	567	595	613	629	639	2,123	5,166
Primary deficit/surplus (–)	345	326	125	155	60	–25	–87	–249	–386	–438	–518	–654	228	–2,017
On-budget deficit/surplus (–)	620	644	466	534	472	431	399	251	117	59	–30	–185	2,301	2,514
Off-budget deficit/surplus (–)	–36	–42	–25	–8	16	25	42	68	92	117	140	169	50	636

Table S–4. Proposed Budget by Category—Continued

(In billions of dollars)

	2016	2017	2018	2019	2020	2021	2022	2023	2024	2025	2026	2027	Totals 2018-2022	Totals 2018-2027
Memorandum, budget authority for discretionary programs:														
Defense	607	646	668	668	668	666	665	679	693	707	722	737	3,335	6,873
Non-defense	560	536	479	464	450	428	419	410	402	394	386	378	2,239	4,209
Total, discretionary funding	1,167	1,182	1,147	1,132	1,118	1,094	1,084	1,089	1,095	1,101	1,108	1,115	5,574	11,081

Table S–5.　Proposed Budget by Category as a Percent of GDP

(As a percent of GDP)

	2016	2017	2018	2019	2020	2021	2022	2023	2024	2025	2026	2027	Totals 2018–2022	Totals 2018–2027
Outlays:														
Discretionary programs:														
Defense	3.2	3.1	3.2	3.2	3.0	2.9	2.7	2.6	2.5	2.5	2.4	2.3	3.0	2.7
Non-defense	3.3	3.2	3.0	2.7	2.4	2.2	2.0	1.8	1.7	1.6	1.5	1.4	2.5	2.0
Subtotal, discretionary programs	6.4	6.3	6.2	5.9	5.5	5.1	4.7	4.4	4.2	4.0	3.9	3.7	5.5	4.8
Mandatory programs:														
Social Security	4.9	4.9	5.0	5.1	5.2	5.2	5.3	5.3	5.4	5.5	5.5	5.6	5.2	5.3
Medicare	3.2	3.1	2.9	3.1	3.2	3.3	3.5	3.5	3.4	3.6	3.7	3.8	3.2	3.4
Medicaid	2.0	2.0	2.0	2.0	2.0	2.0	1.9	1.9	1.8	1.8	1.8	1.7	2.0	1.9
Other mandatory programs	3.0	3.4	2.8	2.9	2.8	2.7	2.7	2.6	2.4	2.4	2.3	2.2	2.8	2.6
Allowance for Obamacare repeal and replacement	....	....	-0.1	-0.1	-0.4	-0.6	-0.6	-0.6	-0.6	-0.6	-0.6	-0.6	-0.4	-0.5
Allowance for infrastructure initiative	....	....	*	0.1	0.2	0.2	0.2	0.1	*	*	*	*	0.1	0.1
Subtotal, mandatory programs	13.2	13.4	12.7	13.1	12.9	12.8	13.0	12.7	12.5	12.6	12.7	12.6	12.9	12.8
Net interest	1.3	1.4	1.6	1.8	1.9	2.1	2.2	2.2	2.2	2.2	2.1	2.1	1.9	2.0
Total outlays	20.9	21.2	20.5	20.7	20.3	20.0	19.9	19.4	18.9	18.9	18.7	18.4	20.3	19.6
Receipts:														
Individual income taxes	8.4	8.7	9.2	9.2	9.3	9.4	9.5	9.5	9.6	9.7	9.8	9.9	9.3	9.5
Corporation income taxes	1.6	1.7	1.8	1.8	1.8	1.7	1.7	1.7	1.6	1.6	1.6	1.6	1.8	1.7
Social insurance and retirement receipts:														
Social Security payroll taxes	4.4	4.5	4.5	4.4	4.4	4.4	4.4	4.4	4.4	4.4	4.5	4.4	4.4	4.4
Medicare payroll taxes	1.3	1.3	1.4	1.4	1.4	1.4	1.4	1.4	1.4	1.4	1.4	1.4	1.4	1.4
Unemployment insurance	0.3	0.3	0.2	0.2	0.2	0.2	0.2	0.2	0.2	0.2	0.2	0.2	0.2	0.2
Other retirement	0.1	0.1	0.1	0.1	0.1	0.1	0.1	0.1	0.1	0.1	0.1	0.1	0.1	0.1
Excise taxes	0.5	0.5	0.5	0.5	0.5	0.4	0.4	0.4	0.4	0.4	0.4	0.4	0.5	0.4
Estate and gift taxes	0.1	0.1	0.1	0.1	0.1	0.1	0.1	0.1	0.1	0.1	0.1	0.1	0.1	0.1
Customs duties	0.2	0.2	0.2	0.2	0.2	0.2	0.2	0.2	0.2	0.2	0.2	0.2	0.2	0.2
Deposits of earnings, Federal Reserve System	0.6	0.5	0.4	0.3	0.2	0.2	0.3	0.3	0.3	0.3	0.3	0.3	0.3	0.3
Other miscellaneous receipts	0.2	0.3	0.3	0.3	0.3	0.2	0.2	0.2	0.2	0.2	0.2	0.2	0.3	0.2
Allowance for Obamacare repeal and replacement	....	....	-0.3	-0.3	-0.4	-0.4	-0.5	-0.4	-0.4	-0.4	-0.4	-0.4	-0.4	-0.4
Total receipts	17.8	18.1	18.3	18.2	18.1	18.0	18.1	18.1	18.2	18.2	18.3	18.4	18.1	18.2
Deficit/surplus (–)	**3.2**	**3.1**	**2.2**	**2.5**	**2.2**	**2.0**	**1.8**	**1.3**	**0.8**	**0.6**	**0.4**	**-0.1**	**2.1**	**1.4**
Net interest	1.3	1.4	1.6	1.8	1.9	2.1	2.2	2.2	2.2	2.1	2.1	2.1	1.9	2.0
Primary deficit/surplus (–)	1.9	1.7	0.6	0.7	0.3	-0.1	-0.4	-1.0	-1.4	-1.6	-1.8	-2.1	0.2	-0.7
On-budget deficit/surplus (–)	3.4	3.4	2.3	2.5	2.1	1.9	1.6	1.0	0.4	0.2	-0.1	-0.6	2.1	1.1
Off-budget deficit/surplus (–)	-0.2	-0.2	-0.1	-*	0.1	0.1	0.2	0.3	0.3	0.4	0.5	0.5	*	0.2

Table S–5. Proposed Budget by Category as a Percent of GDP—Continued

(As a percent of GDP)

	2016	2017	2018	2019	2020	2021	2022	2023	2024	2025	2026	2027	Totals 2018-2022	Totals 2018-2027
Memorandum, budget authority for discretionary programs:														
Defense	3.3	3.4	3.3	3.2	3.0	2.9	2.7	2.7	2.6	2.5	2.4	2.4	3.0	2.8
Non-defense	3.0	2.8	2.4	2.2	2.0	1.9	1.7	1.6	1.5	1.4	1.3	1.2	2.0	1.7
Total, discretionary funding	6.3	6.2	5.7	5.4	5.1	4.7	4.5	4.3	4.1	3.9	3.7	3.6	5.1	4.5

*0.05 percent of GDP or less.

Table S–6. Mandatory and Receipt Proposals

(Deficit increases (+) or decreases (–) in millions of dollars)

	2017	2018	2019	2020	2021	2022	2023	2024	2025	2026	2027	Totals 2018-2022	Totals 2018-2027
Agriculture:													
Farm Bill savings:													
Limit crop insurance premium subsidy to $40,000	......	......	–1,552	–1,620	–1,815	–1,826	–1,845	–1,856	–1,885	–1,897	–1,920	–6,813	–16,218
Limit eligiblity for agricultural commodity payments to $500,000 Adjusted Gross Income (AGI)	......	–72	–60	–77	–73	–71	–67	–64	–60	–56	–53	–353	–653
Limit Crop Insurance eligibility to $500,000 AGI	......	......	–34	–35	–40	–42	–45	–49	–53	–58	–64	–151	–420
Eliminate Harvest Price Option for Crop Insurance	......	......	–1,212	–1,251	–1,314	–1,325	–1,335	–1,353	–1,365	–1,378	–1,390	–5,103	–11,924
Streamline conservation programs	......	–84	–210	–272	–319	–402	–560	–716	–886	–1,072	–1,234	–1,287	–5,755
Eliminate small programs	......	–111	–304	–313	–339	–335	–335	–335	–335	–335	–335	–1,402	–3,077
Total Farm Bill savings	......	–267	–3,372	–3,568	–3,900	–4,001	–4,188	–4,373	–4,584	–4,797	–4,996	–15,108	–38,046
Establish Food Safety and Inspection Service (FSIS) user fee	......	......	–660	–660	–660	–660	–660	–660	–660	–660	–660	–2,640	–5,940
Establish Animal Plant and Health Inspection Service (APHIS) user fee	......	–20	–20	–20	–20	–20	–20	–20	–20	–20	–20	–100	–200
Establish Grain Inspection, Packers, and Stock-yards Administration (GIPSA) user fee	......	–30	–30	–30	–30	–30	–30	–30	–30	–30	–30	–150	–300
Establish Agricultural Marketing Service (AMS) user fee	......	–20	–20	–20	–20	–20	–20	–20	–20	–20	–20	–100	–200
Eliminate interest payments to electric & telecommunications utilities	......	–131	–136	–136	–140	–142	–137	–138	–139	–139	–139	–685	–1,377
Eliminate the Rural Economic Development Program	......	–6	–154	–158	–159	......					–477	–477	
Total, Agriculture	......	–474	–4,392	–4,592	–4,929	–4,873	–5,055	–5,241	–5,453	–5,666	–5,865	–19,260	–46,540
Education:													
Create single income-driven student loan repayment plan [1]	......	–1,685	–3,333	–5,317	–6,830	–8,141	–9,060	–9,972	–10,394	–10,726	–10,946	–25,306	–76,404
Eliminate subsidized student loans	......	–1,052	–2,157	–3,098	–3,791	–4,199	–4,499	–4,744	–4,960	–5,145	–5,228	–14,297	–38,873
Eliminate Public Service Loan Forgiveness	......	–859	–1,466	–2,179	–2,679	–3,030	–3,263	–3,493	–3,575	–3,491	–3,436	–10,213	–27,471
Eliminate account maintenance fee payments to guaranty agencies	......	–443	......									–443	–443
Support Year-Round Pell grants	......	81	314	322	327	332	338	344	350	356	361	1,376	3,125
Reallocate mandatory Pell funding to support Year-Round Pell Grants	......	–81	–314	–322	–327	–332	–338	–344	–350	–356	–361	–1,376	–3,125
Total, Education	......	–4,038	–6,956	–10,594	–13,300	–15,370	–16,823	–18,209	–18,930	–19,362	–19,609	–50,259	–143,192
Energy:													
Reduce Strategic Petroleum Reserve by half	......	–500	–500	–552	–1,390	–1,426	–1,489	–1,519	–1,549	–3,793	–3,868	–4,368	–16,586
Restart Nuclear Waste Fund Fee in 2020	......	......	......	–381	–381	–382	–382	–382	–382	–382	–382	–1,144	–3,054
Repeal borrowing authority for Western Area Power Administration (WAPA)	......	–610	–900	–1,095	–660	–725	–235	–50	–50	–50	–50	–3,990	–4,425

Table S–6. Mandatory and Receipt Proposals—Continued

(Deficit increases (+) or decreases (–) in millions of dollars)

	2017	2018	2019	2020	2021	2022	2023	2024	2025	2026	2027	Totals 2018-2022	Totals 2018-2027
Divest Southwestern Power Administration transmission assets	......	......	–13	......	......	......	......	......	......	......	......	–13	–13
Divest WAPA transmission assets	......	......	–580	......	......	......	......	......	......	......	......	–580	–580
Divest Bonneville Power Administration transmission assets	......	......	–1,821	–396	–386	–386	–386	–386	–386	–386	–386	–2,989	–4,919
Total, Energy	......	–1,110	–3,814	–2,424	–2,817	–2,919	–2,492	–2,337	–2,367	–4,611	–4,686	–13,084	–29,576
Health and Human Services:													
Reform Medicaid	......	......	......	–10,000	–20,000	–40,000	–60,000	–80,000	–105,000	–130,000	–165,000	–70,000	–610,000
Extend Children's Health Insurance Program (CHIP) funding through 2019 [2]	......	–2,359	–3,365	159	–250	......	......	......	......	......	......	–5,815	–5,815
Repeal the Independent Payment Advisory Board (IPAB)	......	......	......	......	......	......	1,040	1,471	1,583	1,700	1,828	......	7,621
Improve the Medicare appeals system	......	127	127	127	127	127	127	127	127	127	127	635	1,270
Improve 340B program integrity	......	......	......	......	......	......	......	......	......	......	......	......	......
Prohibit governmental discrimination against health care providers that refuse to cover abortion	......	......	......	......	......	......	......	......	......	......	......	......	......
Interactions	......	–20	......	17	13	2	–3	–3	–5	–3	–4	12	–6
Strengthen Child Support Enforcement and Establishment	......	–22	–35	–54	–68	–85	–86	–87	–90	–90	–91	–264	–708
Establish a Child Support Technology Fund	......	–110	–122	–120	–121	–136	–43	–48	–55	–36	–42	–609	–833
Shift Social Services Block Grant (SSBG) expenditures to Foster Care and Permanency	......	18	22	23	23	23	23	23	23	23	23	109	224
Extend certain Medicare Access and CHIP Reauthorization Act of 2015 (MACRA) programs through 2019:													
Extend Health Centers	......	1,439	3,346	2,161	254	......	......	......	......	......	......	7,200	7,200
Extend the National Health Service Corps	......	62	248	232	56	16	6	......	......	......	......	614	620
Extend Teaching Health Centers Graduate Medical Education	......	60	60	......	......	......	......	......	......	......	......	120	120
Extend Family to Family Health Information Centers	......	1	4	4	1	......	......	......	......	......	......	10	10
Extend the Maternal, Infant, and Early Childhood Home Visiting Program	......	16	112	316	268	68	20	......	......	......	......	780	800
Extend the Special Diabetes Program for the National Institutes of Health and the Indian Health Service	......	180	266	111	30	8	4	2	......	......	......	595	601
Extend Medicare Enrollment Assistance Programs	......	18	32	18	6	2	......	......	......	......	......	76	76
Extend Abstinence Education and Personal Responsibility Education Program	......	3	88	116	54	10	1	5	......	......	......	271	277
Extend Health Profession Opportunity Grants	......	3	45	75	39	7	......	......	......	......	......	169	169
Total Health and Human Services	......	–584	828	–6,815	–19,568	–39,958	–58,911	–78,510	–103,417	–128,279	–163,159	–66,097	–598,374

Table S-6. Mandatory and Receipt Proposals—Continued

(Deficit increases (+) or decreases (−) in millions of dollars)

	2017	2018	2019	2020	2021	2022	2023	2024	2025	2026	2027	Totals 2018-2022	Totals 2018-2027
Homeland Security:													
Extend expiring Customs and Border Protection (CBP) fees	....	....	....	....	....	....	....	....	....	−3,931	−4,143	....	−8,074
Increase Customs user fees	....	−7	−9	−12	−19	−26	−38	−46	−52	−66	−78	−73	−353
Increase immigration user fees	....	....	....	....	....	....	....	....	....	....	....	....	....
Establish Electronic Visa Update System user fee [2]	....	....	....	....	....	....	....	....	....	....	....	....	....
Reform the National Flood Insurance Program	....	−95	−301	−509	−730	−971	−1,076	−1,141	−1,260	−1,375	−1,432	−2,606	−8,890
Authorize mandatory outlays for U.S. Coast Guard Continuation Pay	....	3	9	28	31	33	34	35	36	37	38	104	284
Eliminate BrandUSA; make revenue available to CBP [2]	....	62	70	78	....	....	....	....	....	....	....	210	210
Transfer Electronic System for Travel Authorization receipts to International Trade Administration [2]	....	....	....	....	....	....	....	....	....	....	....	....	....
Total, Homeland Security	....	−36	−231	−415	−718	−964	−1,080	−1,152	−1,276	−5,335	−5,615	−2,365	−16,823
Interior:													
Lease oil and gas in the Arctic National Wildlife Refuge (ANWR)	....	....	....	....	....	−400	−500	....	....	−400	−500	−400	−1,800
Repeal Gulf of Mexico Energy Security Act (GOMESA) State payments	....	−272	−327	−344	−366	−376	−375	−375	−375	−375	−375	−1,685	−3,560
Cancel Southern Nevada Public Land Management Act (SNPLMA) balances	....	−83	−69	−78	....	....	....	....	....	....	....	−230	−230
Repeal enhanced geothermal payments to counties	....	−3	−3	−3	−4	−4	−4	−4	−4	−4	−4	−17	−37
Reauthorize the Federal Land Transaction Facilitation Act	....	−5	−6	−9	−12	−3	....	....	....	....	....	−35	−35
Total, Interior	....	−363	−405	−434	−382	−783	−879	−379	−379	−779	−879	−2,367	−5,662
Labor:													
Establish a paid parental leave program:													
Provide paid parental leave benefits [2]	....	709	709	2,420	1,644	1,868	2,109	2,172	2,296	2,415	2,160	7,350	18,502
Establish an Unemployment Insurance (UI) solvency standard [2]	....	....	....	−758	−1,894	−2,568	−1,045	−1,833	−1,072	−1,488	−2,254	−5,220	−12,912
Improve UI program integrity [2]	....	−94	−215	−251	−249	−243	−211	−253	−249	−241	−228	−1,052	−2,234
Provide for Reemployment Services and Eligibility Assessments [2]	....	....	−88	−541	−562	−522	−411	−413	−493	−499	−519	−1,713	−4,048
Total, establish a paid parental leave program	....	615	406	870	−1,061	−1,465	442	−327	482	187	−841	−635	−692
Improve Pension Benefit Guaranty Corporation (PBGC) solvency	....	−1,196	−1,202	−1,210	−1,294	−1,507	−1,625	−1,705	−1,546	−2,238	−2,335	−6,409	−15,858
Accelerate PBGC premium payment	....	....	....	....	....	....	....	....	3,088	−3,088	−5,005	....	−5,005
Total, Labor	....	−581	−796	−340	−2,355	−2,972	−1,183	−2,032	2,024	−5,139	−8,181	−7,044	−21,555

Table S–6. Mandatory and Receipt Proposals—Continued

(Deficit increases (+) or decreases (-) in millions of dollars)

	2017	2018	2019	2020	2021	2022	2023	2024	2025	2026	2027	Totals 2018-2022	Totals 2018-2027
Transportation:													
Air Traffic Control:													
Reform Air Traffic Control [2]	....	....	....	....	14,391	14,976	15,627	16,382	17,302	18,073	18,881	29,367	115,632
Outlay savings from discretionary cap adjustment					-8,786	-9,669	-10,058	-10,293	-10,407	-10,407	-10,407	-18,455	-70,027
Reform Essential Air Service [2]					52	....	....	....	....	....	....	52	52
Assume Highway Trust Fund outlays conform to baseline levels of Highway Trust Fund revenues	....	367	637	173	-919	-5,546	-15,164	-16,833	-18,156	-19,436	-20,399	-5,288	-95,276
Total, Transportation	....	367	637	173	4,738	-239	-9,595	-10,744	-11,261	-11,770	-11,925	5,676	-49,619
Treasury:													
Provide authority for Bureau of Engraving and Printing to construct new facility [2]		-15	-74	-3	5	-314	5	14	3	165	-494	-401	-708
Veterans Affairs:													
Continue the Veterans Choice Program		718	1,593	2,469	3,056	3,437	3,500	3,500	3,500	3,500	3,500	11,273	28,773
Cap Post–9/11 GI Bill Flight Training		-42	-43	-46	-48	-50	-52	-54	-56	-59	-61	-229	-511
Extend round-down of cost-of-living adjustments (COLAs)		-20	-66	-127	-182	-235	-295	-347	-403	-466	-536	-630	-2,677
Modernize Individual Unemployability		-3,205	-3,394	-3,582	-3,773	-3,968	-4,166	-4,369	-4,576	-4,787	-5,002	-17,922	-40,822
Total, Veterans Affairs		-2,549	-1,910	-1,286	-947	-816	-1,013	-1,270	-1,535	-1,812	-2,099	-7,508	-15,237
Corps of Engineers:													
Divest Washington Aqueduct				-119							....	-119	-119
Reform inland waterways financing [2]	....	-108	-107	-106	-105	-104	-103	-103	-101	-100	-100	-530	-1,037
Total, Corps of Engineers	....	-108	-107	-225	-105	-104	-103	-103	-101	-100	-100	-649	-1,156
Environmental Protection Agency:													
Expand use of pesticide licensing fees	....	5	4	4	4	4	3	2	1	1	1	21	29
Office of Personnel Management (OPM):													
Reduce Federal retirement benefits:													
Eliminate Federal Employee Retirement System COLA; reduce Civil Service Retirement System COLA by 0.5%		-524	-1,187	-1,892	-2,657	-3,481	-4,369	-5,322	-6,344	-7,432	-8,591	-9,740	-41,799
Other Federal retirement changes		-1,875	-2,134	-3,055	-2,617	-3,298	-3,620	-3,943	-4,383	-4,841	-5,280	-12,979	-35,046
Increase Employee Contributions:													
Increase employee contributions to 50% of cost with 6-year phase-in (1% per year) [2]		-1,719	-3,227	-4,810	-6,372	-7,959	-9,537	-9,568	-9,599	-9,624	-9,640	-24,087	-72,055
Intragovernmental effects of OPM proposals (non-scoreable):													
Loss of mandatory offsetting receipts from OPM proposals	....	....	12,295	13,957	15,779	17,425	19,050	19,166	19,280	19,384	19,472	59,456	155,808

Table S-6. Mandatory and Receipt Proposals—Continued

(Deficit increases (+) or decreases (–) in millions of dollars)

	2017	2018	2019	2020	2021	2022	2023	2024	2025	2026	2027	Totals 2018-2022	Totals 2018-2027
Discretionary effect of OPM proposals	....	....	–6,657	–7,230	–7,826	–8,265	–8,624	–8,290	–7,966	–7,650	–7,341	–29,978	–69,849
Total, Office of Personnel Management	....	–4,117	–910	–3,031	–3,692	–5,578	–7,100	–7,957	–9,012	–10,163	–11,380	–17,329	–62,941
Other Independent Agencies:													
Federal Communications Commission:													
Enact Spectrum License User Fee		–50	–150	–300	–450	–500	–500	–500	–500	–500	–500	–1,450	–3,950
Reform the Postal Service		–2,807	–4,685	–4,871	–4,791	–4,923	–4,904	–4,913	–4,795	–4,676	–4,655	–22,077	–46,020
Restructure the Consumer Financial Protection Bureau		–145	–650	–683	–706	–726	–745	–764	–784	–804	–826	–2,910	–6,833
Eliminate the Securities and Exchange Commission Reserve Fund		....	–50	–50	–50	–50	–50	–50	–50	–50	–50	–200	–450
Mandatory effects of agency eliminations		1	....	....	....	–1	....						
Total, Other Independent Agencies		–3,001	–5,535	–5,904	–5,997	–6,200	–6,199	–6,227	–6,129	–6,030	–6,031	–26,639	–57,255
Cross-cutting reforms:													
Repeal and replace Obamacare [2]		25,000	30,000	–5,000	–30,000	–35,000	–40,000	–40,000	–50,000	–50,000	–55,000	–15,000	–250,000
Implement an infrastructure initiative		5,000	25,000	40,000	50,000	40,000	20,000	10,000	5,000	5,000	....	160,000	200,000
Reform welfare programs:													
Reform Supplemental Nutrition Assistance Program (SNAP)		–4,637	–7,627	–13,990	–16,928	–21,130	–24,871	–24,634	–25,714	–26,135	–25,266	–64,312	–190,932
Establish a SNAP authorized retailer application fee		–252	–246	–241	–236	–230	–230	–230	–230	–230	–230	–1,205	–2,355
Eliminate SSBG		–1,411	–1,683	–1,700	–1,700	–1,700	–1,700	–1,700	–1,700	–1,700	–1,700	–8,194	–16,694
Reduce Temporary Assistance for Needy Families (TANF) block grant		–1,218	–1,491	–1,550	–1,582	–1,615	–1,632	–1,632	–1,632	–1,632	–1,632	–7,456	–15,616
Provide funding for welfare research and Census Bureau Survey of Income and Program Participation, transferred from TANF													
Eliminate TANF Contingency Fund		–567	–608	–608	–608	–608	–608	–608	–608	–608	–608	–2,999	–6,039
Require Social Security Number (SSN) for Child Tax Credit & Earned Income Tax Credit [2]		–449	–4,512	–4,447	–4,358	–4,309	–4,296	–4,373	–4,460	–4,555	–4,652	–18,075	–40,411
Total, reform welfare programs		–8,534	–16,167	–22,536	–25,412	–29,592	–33,337	–33,177	–34,344	–34,860	–34,088	–102,241	–272,047
Reform disability programs and test new approaches:													
Test new approaches to increase labor force participation		100	100	100	100	100	–2,494	–5,069	–9,332	–13,809	–18,627	500	–48,831
Reinstate the reconsideration review stage in 10 States		....	71	–10	–59	–526	–246	–263	–305	–354	–376	–524	–2,068
Reduce 12 month retroactive Disability Insurance benefits to six months		–113	–643	–797	–951	–1,043	–1,112	–1,191	–1,272	–1,349	–1,430	–3,547	–9,901
Create sliding scale for multi-recipient Supplemental Security Income families		–743	–827	–861	–882	–956	–906	–862	–955	–979	–1,002	–4,269	–8,973

Table S-6. Mandatory and Receipt Proposals—Continued

(Deficit increases (+) or decreases (-) in millions of dollars)

												Totals	
	2017	2018	2019	2020	2021	2022	2023	2024	2025	2026	2027	2018-2022	2018-2027
Create a probationary period for Administrative Law Judges (ALJs)	....	....	....	....	....	....	....	....	....	....	....	....	....
Eliminate Workers Compensation Reverse Offsets	....	....	–3	–8	–12	–16	–19	–22	–25	–28	–31	–39	–164
Offset overlapping unemployment and disability payments [2]	....	....	–58	–249	–329	–324	–319	–323	–323	–296	–317	–960	–2,538
Total, reform disability programs and test new approaches		–756	–1,360	–1,825	–2,133	–2,765	–5,096	–7,730	–12,212	–16,815	–21,783	–8,839	–72,475
Reduce improper payments:													
Reduce improper payments Government-wide			–719	–1,482	–2,383	–4,288	–4,549	–9,652	–20,480	–38,024	–57,633	–8,872	–139,210
Allow Government-wide use of CBP entry/exit data to prevent improper payments				–1	–5	–11	–20	–26	–31	–40	–43	–17	–177
Use Death Master File to prevent improper payments													
Authorize Social Security Administration (SSA) to use all collection tools to recover funds			–2	–2	–3	–4	–4	–5	–5	–5	–11	–11	–41
Hold fraud facilitators liable for overpayments				–1	–1	–1	–1	–1	–1	–1	–1	–3	–8
Increase overpayment collection threshold for Old Age, Survivors, and Disability Insurance													
Exclude SSA debts from discharge in bankruptcy		–8	–26	–43	–59	–77	–93	–107	–135	–144	–156	–213	–848
Allow SSA to use commercial database to verify real property		–9	–18	–23	–29	–34	–36	–38	–40	–43	–45	–113	–315
Increase oversight of paid tax return preparers [2]		–12	–28	–44	–53	–60	–69	–70	–68	–76	–79	–197	–559
Provide more flexible authority for the Internal Revenue Service to address correctable errors [2]		–14	–31	–35	–38	–42	–47	–50	–55	–61	–66	–160	–439
Total, reduce improper payments		–73	–885	–1,695	–2,636	–4,584	–4,889	–10,020	–20,889	–38,470	–58,111	–9,873	–142,252
Reform the medical liability system [2]		–179	–1,097	–1,928	–3,308	–4,827	–6,541	–8,082	–9,114	–9,642	–10,295	–11,339	–55,013
Reform financial regulation and prevent taxpayer-funded bailouts			–2,400	–3,000	–3,400	–4,300	–4,400	–4,300	–4,300	–4,400	–4,500	–13,100	–35,000
Conduct spectrum auctions below 6 gigahertz				–300	–300						–6,000	–600	–6,600
Eliminate allocations to the Housing Trust Fund and Capital Magnet Fund [2]		–194	–104	–177	–247	–321	–335	–348	–367	–375	–378	–1,044	–2,846
Authorize additional Afghan Special Immigrant Visas		15	20	20	18	18	18	16	15	16	16	91	172
Modify TRICARE Pharmacy fees (includes non-scoreable accrual effect)		293	209	161	117	102	51	29	–49	–93	–187	881	632
Extend Joint Committee mandatory sequestration									8,361	–20,341	–27,435	....	–39,415

Table S-6. Mandatory and Receipt Proposals—Continued

(Deficit increases (+) or decreases (–) in millions of dollars)

	2017	2018	2019	2020	2021	2022	2023	2024	2025	2026	2027	Totals 2018-2022	Totals 2018-2027
Total, cross-cutting reforms	....	20,571	33,216	3,720	-17,301	-41,270	-74,529	-93,612	-117,899	-169,980	-217,761	-1,063	-674,845
Total, mandatory and receipt proposals	....	**3,967**	**9,555**	**-32,168**	**-67,365**	**-122,356**	**-184,954**	**-227,758**	**-275,731**	**-368,861**	**-457,782**	**-208,367**	**-1,723,454**

[1] The single income-driven repayment plan proposal has sizeable interactive effects with the proposals to eliminate subsidized loans and Public Service Loan Forgiveness. These effects, $7.4 billion over 10 years, are included in the single income-driven repayment plan subtotal.

[2] The estimates for this proposal include effects on receipts. The receipt effects included in the totals above are as follows:

	2017	2018	2019	2020	2021	2022	2023	2024	2025	2026	2027	Totals 2018-2022	Totals 2018-2027
Extend Children's Health Insurance Program (CHIP) funding through 2019	....	49	-219	-367	-67	....	....	....	....	....	....	-604	-604
Establish Electronic Visa Update System user fee	....	-27	-27	-31	-28	-29	-28	-31	-28	-29	-28	-142	-286
Eliminate BrandUSA; make revenue available to CBP	....	162	170	178	....	....	....	....	....	....	....	510	510
Transfer Electronic System for Travel Authorization receipts to International Trade Administration	....	-162	-171	-178	-185	-193	-200	-208	-215	-223	-230	-889	-1,965
Provide paid parental leave benefits	....	....	....	....	-916	-962	-971	-1,158	-1,264	-1,365	-1,459	-1,878	-8,095
Establish an Unemployment Insurance (UI) solvency standard	....	....	....	-758	-1,894	-2,568	-1,045	-1,833	-1,072	-1,488	-2,254	-5,220	-12,912
Improve UI program integrity	....	....	4	8	23	42	86	57	81	102	132	77	535
Provide for Reemployment Services and Eligibility Assessments	....	....	-1	....	18	89	238	269	229	264	284	106	1,390
Reform Air Traffic Control	....	....	....	....	14,391	14,976	15,627	16,382	17,302	18,073	18,881	29,367	115,632
Reform Essential Air Service	....	....	....	....	129	130	132	133	134	136	137	259	931
Authority for Bureau of Engraving and Printing to construct new facility	....	-15	-74	-3	5	-314	5	14	3	165	-494	-401	-708
Reform inland waterways financing	....	-108	-107	-106	-105	-104	-103	-103	-101	-100	-100	-530	-1,037
Increase employee contributions to 50% of cost with 6-year phase-in (1% per year)	....	-1,719	-3,227	-4,810	-6,372	-7,959	-9,537	-9,568	-9,599	-9,624	-9,640	-24,087	-72,055
Repeal and replace Obamacare	....	55,000	60,000	85,000	100,000	105,000	115,000	120,000	120,000	120,000	120,000	405,000	1,000,000
Require Social Security Number (SSN) for Child Tax Credit & Earned Income Tax Credit	....	-298	-1,176	-1,194	-1,228	-1,261	-1,313	-1,381	-1,455	-1,526	-1,618	-5,157	-12,450
Offset overlapping unemployment and disability payments	....	....	....	1	3	7	13	18	23	46	36	11	147
Increase oversight of paid tax return preparers	....	-12	-18	-20	-22	-24	-27	-29	-32	-36	-39	-96	-259
Provide more flexible authority for the IRS to address correctable errors	....	-5	-10	-11	-11	-12	-13	-13	-14	-15	-15	-49	-119
Reform the medical liability system	....	-24	-222	-545	-982	-1,468	-2,054	-2,666	-3,053	-3,261	-3,444	-3,241	-17,719
Eliminate allocations to the Housing Trust Fund and Capital Magnet Fund	....	-75	-79	-96	-110	-117	-122	-126	-129	-131	-134	-477	-1,120
Total receipt effects of mandatory proposals	....	52,766	54,843	77,068	102,649	105,233	115,688	119,757	120,810	120,987	120,015	392,559	989,815

Table S–7. Proposed Discretionary Caps for 2018 Budget

(Net budget authority in billions of dollars)

	2017	2018	2019	2020	2021	2022	2023	2024	2025	2026	2027	Totals 2018-2027
Current Law Base Caps:[1]												
Defense	551	549	562	576	590	605	620	636	652	668	685	6,144
Non-Defense	519	516	530	543	556	570	584	599	614	629	645	5,784
Total, Base Current Law Caps	**1,070**	**1,065**	**1,092**	**1,119**	**1,146**	**1,174**	**1,204**	**1,234**	**1,266**	**1,298**	**1,331**	**11,928**
Proposed Base Cap Changes:[2]												
Defense	*+25*	*+54*	*+54*	*+53*	*+52*	*+50*	*+49*	*+47*	*+45*	*+44*	*+42*	*+489*
Non-Defense	*–15*	*–54*	*–77*	*–99*	*–121*	*–144*	*–167*	*–190*	*–213*	*–236*	*–260*	*–1,559*
Total, Base Cap Changes	***+10***	***+****	***–23***	***–46***	***–69***	***–93***	***–118***	***–142***	***–168***	***–193***	***–219***	***–1,070***
Proposed Base Caps:												
Defense[3]	576	603	616	629	642	655	669	683	697	712	727	6,633
Non-Defense	504	462	453	444	435	426	417	409	401	393	385	4,225
Total, Base Caps	**1,080**	**1,065**	**1,069**	**1,073**	**1,077**	**1,081**	**1,086**	**1,092**	**1,098**	**1,105**	**1,112**	**10,858**
Additional Non-Defense (NDD) Cap Reductions for Budget Proposals:[4]												
Air Traffic Control Reform					–10	–10	–10	–10	–10	–10	–10	–73
Federal Employee Retirement Cost Share Reduction			–7	–7	–8	–8	–9	–8	–8	–8	–7	–70
Total, Proposed NDD Cap Reductions			*–7*	*–7*	*–18*	*–19*	*–19*	*–19*	*–18*	*–18*	*–18*	*–143*
Proposed Base Caps with Additional NDD Adjustments:												
Defense[3]	576	603	616	629	642	655	669	683	697	712	727	6,633
Non-Defense	504	462	446	437	417	407	398	390	383	375	367	4,082
Total, Proposed Base Caps	**1,080**	**1,065**	**1,062**	**1,066**	**1,059**	**1,062**	**1,067**	**1,073**	**1,080**	**1,087**	**1,094**	**10,715**
Cap Adjustments:[5]												
Overseas Contingency Operations[6]	89	77	60	43	26	12	12	12	12	12	12	278
Defense	*70*	*65*	*52*	*39*	*24*	*10*	*10*	*10*	*10*	*10*	*10*	*240*
Non-Defense	*19*	*12*	*8*	*4*	*2*	*2*	*2*	*2*	*2*	*2*	*2*	*38*
Emergency Requirements	3											
Program Integrity	2	2	2	2	2	2	2	2	2	2	2	20
Disaster Relief[7]	8	7	7	7	7	7	7	7	7	7	7	68
Total, Cap Adjustments	**101**	**85**	**69**	**52**	**35**	**21**	**21**	**21**	**21**	**21**	**21**	**365**
Total, Discretionary Budget Authority	**1,181**	**1,150**	**1,131**	**1,117**	**1,093**	**1,083**	**1,088**	**1,094**	**1,101**	**1,108**	**1,115**	**11,080**

Table S–7.   Proposed Discretionary Caps for 2018 Budget—Continued

(Net budget authority in billions of dollars)

	2017	2018	2019	2020	2021	2022	2023	2024	2025	2026	2027	Totals 2018-2027
Memorandum—Appropriations Counted Outside of Discretionary Caps:												
21st Century Cures Appropriations[8]	1	1	1	1	*	1	1	*	*	*	....	5
Non-BBEDCA Emergency Funding[9]	–*	–5	....	....	....	....	....	....	....	....	....	–5

* $500 million or less.

[1] The caps presented here are equal to the levels estimated for 2017 through 2021 in the Balanced Budget and Emergency Deficit Control Act of 1985 (BBEDCA) with separate categories of funding for "defense" (or Function 050) and "non-defense" programs. The 2017 caps were revised in the Bipartisan Budget Act of 2015 and the 2018 through 2021 caps include OMB estimates of Joint Committee enforcement (also known as "sequestration"). For 2022 through 2027, programs are assumed to grow at current services growth rates consistent with current law.

[2] The Administration proposed in its March 16 *Blueprint* an increase in the existing defense caps for 2017 and 2018 that is offset with decreases to the non-defense caps. One-half of the 2017 increase ($5 billion of which is classified as Overseas Contingency Operations) is paid for out of non-defense in 2017 while the entire increase in 2018 is paid for out of non-defense. After 2018, the Budget proposes caps through 2027 that reflect an annual 2.1 percent increase for defense programs and an annual two percent (or "2-penny") decrease for non-defense programs.

[3] The defense base cap estimates for 2019-2027 reflect inflated 2018 levels, not a policy judgment. The Administration will determine 2019-2027 defense funding levels in the 2019 Budget, in accordance with the National Security Strategy, National Defense Strategy, and Nuclear Posture Review that are currently under development.

[4] These cap reductions are for reforms in the Budget that would shift the Federal Aviation Administration's air traffic control function to an independent, non-governmental organization beginning in 2021 and reduce Federal agency costs through changes to current civilian employee retirement plans.

[5] The funding amounts below are cap adjustments that are designated pursuant to Section 251(b)(2) of BBEDCA.

[6] The outyear amounts for OCO in the 2018 Budget reflect notional placeholders consistent with a potential transition of certain OCO costs into the base budget while continuing to fund contingency operations. The placeholder amounts do not reflect specific decisions or assumptions about OCO funding in any particular year.

[7] "Disaster Relief" appropriations are amounts designated as such by the Congress provided they are for activities carried out pursuant to a determination under the Robert T. Stafford Disaster Relief and Emergency Assistance Act. These amounts are held to a funding ceiling that is determined one year at a time and OMB currently estimates the 2018 ceiling to be at $7.4 billion. The Administration is requesting $6.8 billion in 2018, but does not explicitly request disaster-designated appropriations in any year after the budget year. A placeholder set at the budget year request level is included in each of the outyears.

[8] The 21st Century Cures Act permitted funds to be appropriated each year and not counted towards the discretionary caps so long as the appropriations were specifically provided for the authorized purposes. These amounts are displayed outside of the discretionary totals for this reason and the levels included through the budget window reflect authorized levels.

[9] The 2018 Budget includes a permanent cancellation of balances of emergency funding in the Department of Energy that were not designated pursuant to BBEDCA. These cancellations are not being re-designated as emergency; therefore no savings are being achieved under the caps nor will the caps be adjusted for these cancellations.

Table S–8. 2018 Discretionary Overview by Major Agency

(Net budget authority in billions of dollars)

	2017 Estimate[1,2]	2018 Request[2]	2018 Request less 2017 Estimate	
			Dollar	Percent
Base Discretionary Funding:				
Cabinet Departments:				
Agriculture[3]	22.7	18.0	–4.6	–20.5%
Commerce	9.2	7.8	–1.5	–15.8%
Defense:[1]				
CR/Enacted for 2017	*521.8*	*574.5*	*+52.8*	*+10.1%*
Adjustment for March Defense Request for 2017	*27.4*	*..........*	*–27.4*	*N/A*
Total, Defense Policy	*549.1*	*574.5*	*+25.4*	*+4.6%*
Education	68.2	59.0	–9.2	–13.5%
Energy	29.7	28.0	–1.7	–5.6%
National Nuclear Security Administration	*12.5*	*13.9*	*+1.4*	*+11.4%*
Other Energy	*17.2*	*14.1*	*–3.1*	*–18.0%*
Health and Human Services[4]	78.0	65.3	–12.7	–16.2%
Homeland Security (DHS):				
DHS excluding 2017 Border Request	*41.3*	*44.1*	*+2.8*	*+6.8%*
March Border Security Request for 2017[1]	*3.0*	*..........*	*–3.0*	*N/A*
Housing and Urban Development (HUD):				
HUD gross total (excluding receipts)	*46.9*	*40.7*	*–6.2*	*–13.2%*
HUD receipts	*–13.2*	*–9.5*	*+3.7*	*N/A*
Interior	13.2	11.7	–1.4	–10.9%
Justice (DOJ):				
DOJ program level (excluding offsets)	*28.8*	*27.7*	*–1.1*	*–3.8%*
DOJ mandatory spending changes (CHIMPs)	*–11.8*	*–11.3*	*+0.5*	*N/A*
Labor	12.1	9.7	–2.4	–19.8%
State and Other International Programs[3]	39.7	28.2	–11.5	–29.1%
Transportation	18.6	16.2	–2.4	–12.7%
Treasury:				
Treasury program level (excluding offsets)	*12.6*	*12.1*	*–0.5*	*–4.1%*
Treasury mandatory spending changes (CHIMPs)	*–0.9*	*–0.9*	*..........*	*N/A*
Veterans Affairs	74.5	78.8	+4.3	+5.8%
Major Agencies:				
Corps of Engineers	6.0	5.0	–1.0	–16.3%
Environmental Protection Agency	8.2	5.7	–2.6	–31.4%
General Services Administration	0.2	0.5	+0.3	N/A
National Aeronautics and Space Administration	19.2	19.1	–0.2	–0.8%

Table S–8.　2018 Discretionary Overview by Major Agency—Continued

(Net budget authority in billions of dollars)

	2017 Estimate[1,2]	2018 Request[2]	2018 Request less 2017 Estimate	
			Dollar	Percent
National Science Foundation	7.4	6.7	–0.8	–10.7%
Small Business Administration	0.9	0.8	–*	–4.9%
Social Security Administration[4]	9.0	9.1	+*	+0.3%
Other Agencies	20.4	17.9	–2.6	–12.5%
2017 Allowance[1]	–13.6	....	+13.6	N/A
Subtotal, Discretionary Base Budget Authority	**1,079.6**	**1,065.0**	**–14.6**	**–1.4%**
Cap Adjustment Funding:				
Overseas Contingency Operations:				
Defense:[1]				
CR / Enacted for 2017	*65.0*	*64.6*	*–0.4*	*–0.6%*
Adjustment for March Defense Request for 2017	*4.7*	....	*–4.7*	*N/A*
Total, Defense Policy	*69.7*	*64.6*	*–5.1*	*–7.3%*
Homeland Security	0.2	....	–0.2	–100.0%
State and Other International Programs	19.2	12.0	–7.2	–37.4%
Subtotal, Overseas Contingency Operations	89.0	76.6	–12.4	–14.0%
Emergency Requirements:				
Agriculture	0.2	....	–0.2	N/A
Housing and Urban Development	0.4	....	–0.4	N/A
Transportation	1.0	....	–1.0	N/A
Corps of Engineers	1.0	....	–1.0	N/A
National Aeronautics and Space Administration	0.1	....	–0.1	N/A
Subtotal, Emergency Requirements	2.7	....	–2.7	N/A
Program Integrity:				
Health and Human Services	0.4	0.4	+0.1	+17.3%
Social Security Administration	1.2	1.5	+0.3	+26.8%
Subtotal, Program Integrity	1.5	1.9	+0.4	+24.5%
Disaster Relief:[5]				
Homeland Security	6.7	6.8	+0.1	+1.2%
Housing and Urban Development	1.4	....	–1.4	N/A
Subtotal, Disaster Relief	8.1	6.8	–1.3	–16.4%
Subtotal, Cap Adjustment Funding	**101.4**	**85.3**	**–16.1**	**–15.9%**
Total, Discretionary Budget Authority	**1,181.0**	**1,150.3**	**–30.7**	**–2.6%**

Table S–8. 2018 Discretionary Overview by Major Agency—Continued

(Net budget authority in billions of dollars)

	2017 Estimate[1,2]	2018 Request[2]	2018 Request less 2017 Estimate	
			Dollar	Percent
Memorandum - Appropriations Counted Outside of Discretionary Caps:				
21st Century Cures Appropriations:[6]				
Health and Human Services	0.9	1.1	+0.2	+21.1%
Non-BBEDCA Emergency Appropriations:				
Agriculture	–*	*	+*	N/A
Energy[7]	....	-4.7	-4.7	N/A

* $50 million or less.

[1] At the time the 2018 Budget was prepared, 2017 appropriations remained incomplete and the 2017 column reflects at the account level enacted full-year and continuing appropriations provided under the Continuing Appropriations Act, 2017 (Division C of Public Law 114-223, as amended by Division A of Public Law 114-254 and amended further by Public Law 115-30) that expired on May 5. In addition, the levels are adjusted to illustratively reflect the current law caps for 2017 and the Administration's March 16 request for additional appropriations for defense and border security, which are included with the levels shown for the Departments of Defense and Homeland Security. The 2017 levels include a further allowance adjustment to reflect the reductions to non-defense programs proposed by the Administration.

[2] Enacted, continuing, and proposed changes in mandatory programs (CHIMPs) are included in both 2017 and 2018.

[3] Funding for Food for Peace Title II Grants is included in the State and Other International Programs total. Although the funds are appropriated to the Department of Agriculture, the funds are administered by the U.S. Agency for International Development.

[4] Funding from the Hospital Insurance and Supplementary Medical Insurance trust funds for administrative expenses incurred by the Social Security Administration that support the Medicare program are included in the Health and Human Services total and not in the Social Security Administration total.

[5] "Disaster Relief" appropriations are amounts designated by the Congress provided they are for activities carried out pursuant to a determination under the Robert T. Stafford Disaster Relief and Emergency Assistance Act. These amounts are held to a funding ceiling that is determined one year at a time and OMB currently estimates the 2018 ceiling to be at $7.4 billion. The Administration is requesting $6.8 billion in 2018.

[6] The 21st Century Cures Act permitted funds to be appropriated each year for certain activities and not counted toward the discretionary caps so long as the appropriations were specifically provided for the authorized purposes. These amounts are displayed outside of the discretionary totals for this reason.

[7] The 2018 Budget proposes to eliminate the Title 17 Innovative Technology Loan Guarantee Program and the Advanced Technology Vehicles Manufacturing Loan Program in the Department of Energy. This proposal includes a permanent cancellation of most of the remaining balances of emergency funding that were not designated pursuant to BBEDCA. These cancellations are not being re-designated as emergency; therefore no savings are being achieved under the caps nor will the caps be adjusted for these cancellations.

Table S–9. Economic Assumptions[1]

(Calendar years)

	Actual		Projections										
	2015	2016	2017	2018	2019	2020	2021	2022	2023	2024	2025	2026	2027
Gross Domestic Product (GDP):													
Nominal level, billions of dollars	18,037	18,566	19,367	20,237	21,197	22,253	23,379	24,563	25,806	27,111	28,483	29,924	31,439
Percent change, nominal GDP, year/year	3.7	2.9	4.3	4.5	4.7	5.0	5.1	5.1	5.1	5.1	5.1	5.1	5.1
Real GDP, percent change, year/year	2.6	1.6	2.3	2.4	2.7	2.9	3.0	3.0	3.0	3.0	3.0	3.0	3.0
Real GDP, percent change, Q4/Q4	1.9	1.9	2.3	2.5	2.8	3.0	3.0	3.0	3.0	3.0	3.0	3.0	3.0
GDP chained price index, percent change, year/year	1.1	1.3	1.9	2.0	2.0	2.0	2.0	2.0	2.0	2.0	2.0	2.0	2.0
Consumer Price Index,[2] percent change, year/year	0.1	1.3	2.6	2.3	2.3	2.3	2.3	2.3	2.3	2.3	2.3	2.3	2.3
Interest rates, percent:[3]													
91-day Treasury bills[4]	*	0.3	0.8	1.5	2.1	2.6	2.9	3.0	3.0	3.0	3.1	3.1	3.1
10-year Treasury notes	2.1	1.8	2.7	3.3	3.4	3.8	3.8	3.8	3.8	3.8	3.8	3.8	3.8
Unemployment rate, civilian, percent[3]	5.3	4.9	4.6	4.4	4.6	4.7	4.8	4.8	4.8	4.8	4.8	4.8	4.8

* 0.05 percent or less.

Note: A more detailed table of economic assumptions appears in Chapter 2, "Economic Assumptions and Interactions with the Budget," in the *Analytical Perspectives* volume of the Budget.

[1] Based on information available as of early March, 2017.

[2] Seasonally adjusted CPI for all urban consumers.

[3] Annual average.

[4] Average rate, secondary market (bank discount basis).

Table S–10. Federal Government Financing and Debt

(Dollar amounts in billions)

	Actual 2016	Estimate										
		2017	2018	2019	2020	2021	2022	2023	2024	2025	2026	2027
Financing:												
Unified budget deficit/surplus (–):												
Primary deficit/surplus (–)	345	326	125	155	60	–25	–87	–249	–386	–438	–518	–654
Net interest	240	276	315	371	428	481	528	567	595	613	629	639
Unified budget deficit/surplus (–)	585	603	440	526	488	456	442	319	209	176	110	–16
As a percent of GDP	3.2%	3.1%	2.2%	2.5%	2.2%	2.0%	1.8%	1.3%	0.8%	0.6%	0.4%	–0.1%
Other transactions affecting borrowing from the public:												
Changes in financial assets and liabilities:[1]												
Change in Treasury operating cash balance	155	–3	......	......	......	......	......	......	......	......	......	......
Net disbursements of credit financing accounts:												
Direct loan and Troubled Asset Relief Program (TARP) equity purchase accounts	83	67	88	81	68	65	61	61	60	60	58	55
Guaranteed loan accounts	16	–9	2	–1	–2	–5	–7	–9	–5	–5	–5	–4
Net purchases of non-Federal securities by the National Railroad Retirement Investment Trust (NRRIT)	*	–1	–1	–1	–1	–1	–1	–1	–1	–1	–1	*
Net change in other financial assets and liabilities[2]	213	......										
Subtotal, changes in financial assets and liabilities	467	54	90	79	64	59	53	51	54	54	52	50
Seigniorage on coins	–1	–1	–1	–1	–1	–1	–1	–1	–1	–1	–1	–1
Total, other transactions affecting borrowing from the public	466	54	89	78	64	59	52	51	54	54	52	50
Total, requirement to borrow from the public (equals change in debt held by the public)	1,051	656	529	604	552	515	494	369	263	229	162	34
Changes in Debt Subject to Statutory Limitation:												
Change in debt held by the public	1,051	656	529	604	552	515	494	369	263	229	162	34
Change in debt held by Government accounts	368	159	210	142	112	96	39	54	76	*	–20	–140
Change in other factors	6	1	2	3	3	2	2	2	2	1	1	2
Total, change in debt subject to statutory limitation	1,425	816	740	749	666	613	535	426	341	230	143	–104
Debt Subject to Statutory Limitation, End of Year:												
Debt issued by Treasury	19,513	20,328	21,067	21,815	22,479	23,091	23,625	24,049	24,389	24,620	24,763	24,658
Adjustment for discount, premium, and coverage[3]	25	27	28	30	31	32	34	35	36	36	36	37
Total, debt subject to statutory limitation[4]	19,538	20,355	21,095	21,844	22,510	23,123	23,658	24,084	24,425	24,656	24,799	24,695
Debt Outstanding, End of Year:												
Gross Federal debt:[5]												
Debt issued by Treasury	19,513	20,328	21,067	21,815	22,479	23,091	23,625	24,049	24,389	24,620	24,763	24,658
Debt issued by other agencies	26	27	26	25	24	23	23	21	20	19	19	18
Total, gross Federal debt	19,539	20,354	21,093	21,840	22,503	23,114	23,647	24,071	24,410	24,639	24,781	24,676
As a percent of GDP	106.1%	106.2%	105.4%	104.3%	102.4%	100.1%	97.5%	94.4%	91.2%	87.6%	83.8%	79.5%

Table S–10. Federal Government Financing and Debt—Continued

(Dollar amounts in billions)

	Actual 2016	Estimate 2017	2018	2019	2020	2021	2022	2023	2024	2025	2026	2027
Held by:												
Debt held by Government accounts	5,372	5,531	5,740	5,883	5,994	6,090	6,130	6,184	6,260	6,260	6,240	6,101
Debt held by the public[6]	14,168	14,824	15,353	15,957	16,509	17,024	17,517	17,887	18,150	18,379	18,541	18,575
As a percent of GDP	77.0%	77.4%	76.7%	76.2%	75.1%	73.7%	72.2%	70.2%	67.8%	65.3%	62.7%	59.8%
Debt Held by the Public Net of Financial Assets:												
Debt held by the public	14,168	14,824	15,353	15,957	16,509	17,024	17,517	17,887	18,150	18,379	18,541	18,575
Less financial assets net of liabilities:												
Treasury operating cash balance	353	350	350	350	350	350	350	350	350	350	350	350
Credit financing account balances:												
Direct loan and TARP equity purchase accounts	1,227	1,294	1,383	1,464	1,532	1,597	1,658	1,719	1,779	1,839	1,897	1,952
Guaranteed loan accounts	28	18	20	19	17	12	5	–4	–9	–14	–19	–23
Government-sponsored enterprise preferred stock	109	109	109	109	109	109	109	109	109	109	109	109
Non-Federal securities held by NRRIT	24	24	22	21	20	19	18	17	17	16	16	15
Other assets net of liabilities	–42	–42	–42	–42	–42	–42	–42	–42	–42	–42	–42	–42
Total, financial assets net of liabilities	1,699	1,753	1,842	1,921	1,985	2,045	2,097	2,149	2,203	2,257	2,310	2,360
Debt held by the public net of financial assets	12,469	13,071	13,511	14,036	14,524	14,979	15,420	15,738	15,947	16,122	16,232	16,215
As a percent of GDP	67.7%	68.2%	67.5%	67.0%	66.1%	64.9%	63.6%	61.7%	59.5%	57.3%	54.9%	52.2%

* $500 million or less.

[1] A decrease in the Treasury operating cash balance (which is an asset) is a means of financing a deficit and therefore has a negative sign. An increase in checks outstanding (which is a liability) is also a means of financing a deficit and therefore also has a negative sign.

[2] Includes checks outstanding, accrued interest payable on Treasury debt, uninvested deposit fund balances, allocations of special drawing rights, and other liability accounts; and, as an offset, cash and monetary assets (other than the Treasury operating cash balance), other asset accounts, and profit on sale of gold.

[3] Consists mainly of debt issued by the Federal Financing Bank (which is not subject to limit), the unamortized discount (less premium) on public issues of Treasury notes and bonds (other than zero-coupon bonds), and the unrealized discount on Government account series securities.

[4] The statutory debt limit is approximately $19,809 billion, as increased after March 15, 2017.

[5] Treasury securities held by the public and zero-coupon bonds held by Government accounts are almost all measured at sales price plus amortized discount or less amortized premium. Agency debt securities are almost all measured at face value. Treasury securities in the Government account series are otherwise measured at face value less unrealized discount (if any).

[6] At the end of 2016, the Federal Reserve Banks held $2,463.5 billion of Federal securities and the rest of the public held $11,704.3 billion. Debt held by the Federal Reserve Banks is not estimated for future years.

OMB CONTRIBUTORS TO THE 2018 BUDGET

The following personnel contributed to the preparation of this publication. Hundreds, perhaps thousands, of others throughout the Government also deserve credit for their valuable contributions.

A

Andrew Abrams
Chandana L. Achanta
Brenda Aguilar
Natalie Ahinakwa
Ruby Ahmed
Shagufta Ahmed
Steve Aitken
Jason Alleman
Victoria Allred
Lois E. Altoft
Jessica C. Anderson
Jessica A. Andreasen
Analisa Archer
David Armitage
Benton T. Arnett
Anna R. Arroyo
Emily Schultz Askew
Lisa L. August
Renee Austin
Kristin B. Aveille
Anjam Aziz

B

Leah G. Babins
Michelle B. Bacon
Jessie W. Bailey
Ally Pregulman Bain
Coalter Baker
Paul W. Baker
Christian Bale
Carol A. Bales
Pratik S. Banjade
Avital Bar-Shalom
Amy C. Barker
Patti A. Barnett
Jody M. Barringer
Sarah O. Bashadi
Amy Batchelor
Jennifer Wagner Bell
Anna M. Bellantoni
Nathaniel Benjamin

Joseph J. Berger
Elizabeth A. Bernhard
Antonia K. Bernhardt
Jamie Berryhill
Kyle Bibby
Emily R. Bilbao
Christopher Biolsi
Samuel J. Black
Robert B. Blair
Daniel Block
Mathew C. Blum
James Boden
Erin Boeke Burke
Cassie L. Boles
Melissa B. Bomberger
William J. Boyd
Mollie Bradlee
Sean W. T. Branchaw
Michael Branson
Alex M. Brant
Joseph F. Breighner
Julie A. Brewer
Andrea M. Brian
Erik G. Brine
Candice M. Bronack
Jonathan M. Brooks
Dustin S. Brown
Sheila Bruce
Michael T. Brunetto
Robert W. Buccigrossi
Nicole J. Buell
Pearl Buenvenida
Tom D. Bullers
Scott H. Burgess
Ben Burnett
John D. Burnim
Meghan K. Burris
John C. Burton
Nicholas S. Burton
Mark Bussow
Dylan W. Byrd

C

Steve E. Cahill
Gregory J. Callanan
Eric Cardoza
Matthew B. Carney
Kerrie Carr
J. Kevin Carroll
William S. S. Carroll
Scott D. Carson
Sean C. Casey
Mary Cassell
James Chase
Nida Chaudhary
Michael Chelen
Anita Chellaraj
Yungchih Chen
Gezime Christian
Michael Clark
Angela Colamaria
William P. Cole
Victoria W. Collin
Debra M. Collins
Kelly T. Colyar
Jose A. Conde
David Connolly
Daniel Consigili
Sara A. Cortez
Drew W. Cramer
Catherine E. Crato
Tyler Overstreet
    Cromer
Rose Crow
Juliana Crump
Craig Crutchfield
David M. Cruz-
    Glaudemans
Lily Cuk
C. Tyler Curtis
William Curtis
Charles R. Cutshall
Ashley Nathanson
    Czin
John (CZ) Czwartacki

D

Veronica Daigle
Nadir Dalal
D. Michael Daly
Rody Damis
Neil B. Danberg
Charlie Dankert
Kristy L. Daphnis
Alexander J. Daumit
Joanne Chow
    Davenport
Kenneth L. Davis
Chad J. Day
Brandon F. DeBruhl
Tasha M. Demps
Paul J. Denaro
Catherine A. Derbes
Chris J. DeRusha
John H. Dick
Darbi S. Dillon
Julie Allen Dingley
Angela M. Donatelli
Paul S. Donohue
Vladik Dorjets
Anjelica B. Dortch
Emma Doyle
Lisa Cash Driskill
Laura E. Duke
Carolyn Dula-Wilson

E

Matthew C. Eanes
Jacqueline A. Easley
Kathryn Edelman
Jeanette Edwards
Emily M. Eelman
Claire Ehmann
Anthony J. Eleftherion
Jeffrey M. Elkin
Christopher J. Elliott
Tonya L. Ellison-Mays
Michelle Enger

Diana F. Epstein
Neal R. Erickson
Edward V. Etzkorn

F

Farnoosh Faezi-Marian
Robert Fairweather
Ladan Fakory
Edna Falk Curtin
Michael C. Falkenheim
Hunter Fang
Kara L. Farley-Cahill
Christine E.
  Farquharson
Kira R. Fatherree
Christopher M. Felix
Russell Ficken
Lesley A. Field
Mary S. Fischietto
E Holly Fitter
John J. Fitzpatrick
Tana Fitzpatrick
Darlene B. Fleming
Carolyn Fleming-
  Williams
Nicholas A. Fraser
Jeffrey K. Freeland

G

Andrew J. Galkowski
Arianne J. Gallagher
Ryan J. Galloway
Christopher D.
  Gamache
Mar Gamboa
Amy T. Gao
Mathias A. Gardner
Marc Garufi
Thomas O. Gates
Roy J. Gelfand
Emily R. Gentile
Paul A. Gill
Brian Gillis
Janelle R. Gingold
Joshua S. Glazer
Andrea L. Goel
Ja'Cia D. Goins
Jeffrey D. Goldstein
Anthony A. Gonzalez
Oscar Gonzalez
Margie Graves
John W. Gray

Robert A. Green
Aron Greenberg
Brandon H. Greene
Justin M. Grimes
Hester C. Grippando
Joe Grogan
Stephanie Grosser
Andrea L. Grossman

H

Michael B. Hagan
Tia Hall
William F. Hamele
Daniel Hanlon
Brian Hanson
Jennifer L. Hanson
Linda W. Hardin
Dionne Hardy
Melanie Harris
Deidre A. Harrison
Paul Harvey
Alyson M. Hatchett
Kyle Hathaway
Laurel S. Havas
Nora K. Hawkins
Nichole M. Hayden
Mark Hazelgren
Noreen Hecmanczuk
John David Henson
Kevin W. Herms
Lindsay Herron
Jim Herz
David G. Hester
Alexander G.
  Hettinger
Gretchen T. Hickey
Michael J. Hickey
Amanda M. Hill
Andrew D. Hire
Tom Hitter
Jennifer E. Hoef
Adam Hoffberg
Stuart Hoffman
Trent W. Holbrook
Troy Holland
Brian C. Holloway
James S. Holm
Kristen T. Honey
Lynette Hornung
Carole House
Rory C. Howe
Grace Hu
Jamie W. Huang

Kathy M. Hudgins
Alexander T. Hunt
Lorraine D. Hunt
James C. Hurban
Veta P. Hurst

I

Adrian B. Ilagan
Tae H. Im
Mason C. Ingram
Janet E. Irwin

J

Brian M. Jacob
Manish Jain
Varun M. Jain
Carol Jenkins
Carol Johnson
Michael D. Johnson
Danielle Y. Jones
Denise Bray Jones
Lisa M. Jones
Othni A. Jones
Thomas J. Jones
Hee Jun

K

Paul A. Kagan
Sandra Kalmus
Daniel S. Kaneshiro
Jacob H. Kaplan
Regina L. Kearney
Daniel J. Keenaghan
Matthew J. Keeneth
Hunter S. Kellett
Nancy B. Kenly
Alper A. Kerman
Saha Khaterzai
Shubha Khot
Paul E. Kilbride
Emily C. Kilcrease
Rachael Y. Kim
Barry King
Emily C. King
Kelly A. Kinneen
David E. Kirkpatrick
Benjamin W. Klay
Robert T. Klein
Chloe Kontos
Andrea G. Korovesis
Kathy Kraninger

Lori A. Krauss
Kristen L. Kruger
Steven B. Kuennen
Joydip Kundu

L

Christopher D. LaBaw
Leonard L. Lainhart
James A. Laity
Lawrence L. Lambert
Daniel LaPlaca
Anthony Larkins
Derek B. Larson
Eric P. Lauer
Jessie L. LaVine
Matthew J. Lawrence
Suzette Lawson
Christopher Leach
Jessica Lee
Karen F. Lee
Susan E. Leetmaa
Bryan León
Annika N. Lescott
Kerrie Leslie
Stuart Levenbach
Malissa C. Levesque
Sheila Lewis
Wendy L. Liberante
Richard Alan
  Lichtenberger
Kristina E. Lilac
Erika Liliedahl
Adam Lipton
Joseph M. Liss
Tsitsi Liywalii
Patrick Locke
Sara R. López
Alexander W. Louie
Adrienne Lucas
Gideon F. Lukens

M

Chi T. Mac
Ryan MacMaster
Claire A. Mahoney
Dominic J. Mancini
Noah S. Mann
Sharon Mar
Celinda A. Marsh
Lexi Marten
Brendan A. Martin
Shelly McAllister

George H. McArdle
Alexander J.
  McClelland
Connor G. McCrone
Timothy D. McCrosson
Anthony W. McDonald
Christine A. McDonald
Katrina A. McDonald
Renford A. McDonald
Kevin E. McGinnis
Kevin J. McKernin
Charlie E. McKiver
Moutray McLaren
William M. McLaren
Robin J. McLaughry
Megan B. McPhaden
William J. McQuaid
William J. Mea
Melissa R. Medeiros
Inna L. Melamed
Patrick J. Mellon
Barbara A. Menard
Flavio Menasce
Jose A. Mendez
P. Thaddeus
  Messenger
Todd Messer
William L. Metzger
Daniel J. Michelson-
  Horowitz
Julie L. Miller
Kimberly Miller
Susan M. Minson
Asma Mirza
Mia Mitchell
Rehana I. Mohammed
Emily A. Mok
Claire Monteiro
Joe Montoni
Zachary Morgan
Kelly Morrison
Joshua A. Moses
James S. Mulligan
Mick Mulvaney
Christian G. Music
Hayley W. Myers
Kimberley L Myers

N

Jennifer M. Nading
Jeptha E. Nafziger
Larry J. Nagl
Anna M. Naimark

Barry Napear
Robert Nassif
Kimberly P. Nelson
Melissa K. Neuman
Joanie F. Newhart
Kimberly Armstrong
  Newman
Anthony (Tony)
  Nguyen
Teresa O. Nguyen
Brian A. Nichols
Tige Nishimoto
Douglas E. Nivens, II
Ross Nodurft
Tim H. Nusraty
Joseph B. Nye

O

Erin O'Brien
Matthew J. O'Kane
Brendan J. O'Meara
Jared Ostermiller

P

Benjamin J. Page
Heather C. Pajak
Jennifer Park
John C. Pasquantino
Neal A. Patel
Tarlika Patel
Terri B. Payne
Marcus Peacock
Falisa L. Peoples-Tittle
Michael A. Perz
David B. Peterson
Andrea M. Petro
Stephen P. Petzinger
Stacey Que-Chi Pham
Carolyn R. Phelps
Karen A. Pica
Kailey Pickitt
Brian K. Pipa
Joseph Pipan
Mark J. Pomponio
Ruxandra Pond
Nancy Potok
Celestine Michelle
  Pressley
Larrimer S. Prestosa
Jamie M. Price
Daniel Proctor
Rob Purdy

Rob Pyron

R

Lucas R. Radzinschi
Latonda Glass Raft
Christopher P. Rahaim
Moshiur Rahman
Maria S. Raphael
Aaron D. Ray
Alex Reed
Meagan E. Reed
Mark A. Reger
Rudolph G. Regner
Paul B. Rehmus
Sean C. Reilly
Thomas M. Reilly
Bryant D. Renaud
Hubbard A. Rhea
Keri A. Rice
Shannon A. Richter
Kyle S. Riggs
Emma K. Roach
Amanda Robbins
Beth Higa Roberts
Kelly M. Roberts
Donovan Robinson
Marshall J. Rodgers
Meredith B. Romley
Eric Rosenfield
Jefferson Rosman
David J. Rowe
Mario Roy
Jaqueline Rudas
Erika H. Ryan

S

Fouad P. Saad
John Asa Saldivar
Alvand A. Salehi
Cesar Xicotencatl
  Sanchez
Mark S. Sandy
Tricia Schmitt
Daniel K. Schory
Nancy E. Schwartz
Mariarosaria
  Sciannameo
Jasmeet K. Seehra
Robert B. Seidner
Douglas Sellers
Shahid N. Shah

Shabnam
  Sharbatoghlie
Dianne Shaughnessy
Sanchez M. Shaun
Paul Shawcross
David Shorkrai
Gary F. Shortencarrier
Sara R. Sills
Samantha E.
  Silverberg
Robert Sivinski
Benjamin J. Skidmore
Jonathan Slemrod
Jack Smalligan
Curtina O. Smith
Stannis M. Smith
Rachel B. Snyderman
Erica Socker
Silvana Solano
Roderic A. Solomon
Amanda R.K. Sousan
Rebecca L. Spavins
Raquel A. Spencer
Sarah Whittle Spooner
Linda Springer
Travis Stalcup
Scott R. Stambaugh
Nora Stein
Lamar R. Stewart
Gary R. Stofko
Terry W. Stratton
Joseph G. Stuntz
Frank Sturges
Thomas J. Suarez
Kathy L. Suber
Alec J Sugarman
Joseph Lee Suh
Kevin J. Sullivan
Jessica L. Sun
Christina Swoope
Katherine M. Sydor
Aaron L. Szabo

T

Jamie R. Taber
John Tambornino
Naomi S. Taransky
Joseph Tawney
Myra L. Taylor
Emma K. Tessier
Amanda L. Thomas
Payton A. Thomas
Will Thomas

Rich Thoreau
Philip Tizzani
Thomas Tobasko
Gia Tonic
Mariel E. Townsend
Gil M. Tran
Donald L. Tuck
Austin Turner
Benjamin J. Turpen

U

Nicholas Ufier
Shraddha A.
   Upadhyaya
Darrell J. Upshaw
Taylor J. Urbanski
Euler V. Uy

V

Matthew J. Vaeth
Cynthia Vallina
Haley Van Dyck
Sarita Vanka
Areletha L. Venson
Alexandra Ventura
Patricia A. Vinkenes
Dean R. Vonk
Russ Vought
Ann M. Vrabel

W

James A. Wade
Brett Waite
Heather V. Walsh
Kan Wang
Tim Wang
Gary Waxman
Bess M. Weaver
Jeffrey A. Weinberg

David Weisshaar
Nathan Wells
Philip R. Wenger
Max W. West
Steve Wetzel
Arnette C. White
Ashley M. White
Catherine E. White
Kamela White
Kim S. White
RaeShawn White
Sherron R. White
Chad S. Whiteman
Katie Whitman
Brian Widuch
Mary Ellen Wiggins
Debra (Debbie) L.
   Williams
Michael B. Williams
Jamie S. Wilson
Ron Wilson

Paul A. Winters
Julia B. Wise
Julie Wise
Elizabeth D. Wolkomir
Minzy Won
Raymond J.M. Wong
Charles E.
   Worthington
Sophia M. Wright
William Wu
Bert Wyman

Y

Melany N. Yeung
David Y. Yi
Elliot Y. Yoon

Z

Bill Zielinski